MATHEMATICS POWER LEARNING
FOR CHILDREN
ACTIVATING THE CONTEXTUAL LEARNER

BOOK TWO

Everard Barrett

CONTEXTUAL MATHEMATICS TEACHING METHODOLOGY

Professor B. Enterprises, Inc.
P. O. Box 2079
Duluth, Georgia 30096
www.profb.com

FIFTH EDITION REVISED

MATHEMATICS POWER LEARNING FOR CHILDREN
ACTIVATING THE CONTEXTUAL LEARNER

Copyrights and acknowledgments

Editor
Everard Barrett

Production Manager
Veda Barrett

Cover Art
Charles J. Berger

Publisher
Professor B Enterprises, Inc.
P. O. Box 2079
Duluth, Georgia 30096
www.profb.com

FIFTH EDITION REVISED

ISBN 1-883324-02-5

Library of Congress Catalog Card Number: 93-92702

Printed in the United States of America

To Him that is able to keep me from falling.

ABOUT THE AUTHOR

Everard Barrett has been an Associate Professor in the Mathematics Department, State University of New York, College at Old Westbury since 1971 and is the president of Professor B Enterprises, Inc. From 1962 to 1971, he taught junior and senior high school mathematics in Brooklyn, New York.

He is the originator of the Contextual Mathematics Teaching Methodology and has conducted numerous interventions in public schools within twelve states of the U.S. since 1973. Results, as substantiated by many statistical analyses, have been consistently strong. Over and over again, he has moved his projects through the cycle of implementation, teachers' feedback, statistical evaluation, and revision.

In June 1976, after three years of experimental work in the Theodore Roosevelt Elementary School, Roosevelt, New York, he broke new educational ground by enabling fifth and sixth grade classes to out-perform (by a wide margin) their ninth grade counterparts on an examination traditionally reserved for the brightest ninth graders (The New York State Ninth Year Algebra Regents Examination) throughout the state. This was subsequently repeated (on two occasions) in P.S. 44, an elementary school within Central Bedford Stuyvesant, Brooklyn, New York.

Professor Barrett was commissioned to a UNESCO mission in mathematics education in St. Lucia, Grenada, and Jamaica at the request of their governments in 1980. Following the World Conference on Education for All in Jomtien, Thailand during March, 1990, he was invited to present his methodology at the first seminar held by the United Nations Development Program (UNDP) in its search for "fresh, theoretically grounded methodologies for addressing fundamental educational requirements" (such as those identified at Jomtien). The one and one-half day session, on "Innovative Approaches to Meeting Basic Learning Needs," was convened at UNDP Headquarters, New York, in January, 1991. Professor Barrett was one of four presenters. Participants were educational specialists and program staff from International Agencies such as UNDP, UNESCO, the World Bank, UNICEF, bilateral agencies, and institutes. The Director of UNESCO's International Institute for Educational Planning (IIEP) attended throughout the duration of the seminar.

The directors of IIEP and UNDP were sufficiently impressed with his methodology to refer him to the Chief of the Regional Bureau for Latin America and the Caribbean, for the purpose of initiating a UNDP-sponsored project in Jamaica, W.I.

The pilot phase of the Project was completed during Summer, 1992. After receiving training in Professor Barrett's methodology, sixteen mathematics lecturers from local teachers' colleges enabled 94% of 265 practicing primary teachers to pass a qualifying Primary Mathematics Examination, which the vast majority of them had failed repeatedly. The teachers received instruction from the lecturers for five days per week, through five weeks. The highest passing rate ever achieved previously (since 1981), by a similar population of primary teachers under the same circumstances, was only 20%. In fact, the highest passing rate ever achieved previously by a population of mixed abilities was 60%.

This impressive performance in the summer pilot has earned Professor Barrett an extension of the Project for two years. As this intervention continues, the remaining population of practicing teachers unqualified to teach mathematics will be reduced to an insignificantly small number. A national problem will have been solved.

TABLE OF CONTENTS

PREFACE

We have been firmly committed to the concept that successful pedagogy for mathematical competence in young learners can only evolve from large concentrations of time, energy, and dedication in elementary classrooms. On a yearly basis, since 1973, we have gone, full cycle, from intensive implementation and practice of the methodology, to thorough reflection upon its impact (supplemented by teachers' feedback), and then to meticulous revision.

Consequently, we have paid our dues, and our efforts have been rewarded with the development of an original pedagogy and program which guarantees accelerated learning of mathematics to virtually all children.

In order to establish credibility for our claim that virtually all children can learn mathematics successfully, we have accumulated, through these years, a huge quantity of statistical analyses. All of them show enormous growth in mathematical achievement, over relatively short periods of time, in schools which span the socio-economic spectrum. Over and over again, mean grade equivalent scores in participating elementary schools have grown from 1.5 to 3 years per year of instruction, after the first five to eight months of staff development in our methodology. Through the past twenty years, we have consistently enabled teachers to deliver mental, rapid-response knowledge of the higher addition and subtraction facts to first graders (and multiplication facts, up to five times, in some instances); as well as long division (with three-place divisors and six-place dividends) to second graders. In fact, ours is the only intervention, nationwide, which has enabled fifth and sixth grade classes, from the very lowest of socio-economic environments, to perform competently on the same exam in Algebra I, traditionally reserved for the brightest ninth graders throughout the state. This was done on three different occasions (in different school years).

How did all this happen? What were the compelling awarenesses which so effectively transformed the teachers' perspectives on the teaching of mathematics and, consequently, their pedagogical strategies and techniques in their own classrooms?

The philosophical and psychological foundations of our methodology are presented in the following reference:

> Barrett, E. (1992). "Teaching Mathematics through Context: Unleashing the Power of the Contextual Learner." In R. Tobias, ed., Nurturing At-Risk Youth in Math and Science. Bloomington, IN: National Educational Service.

However, we may briefly state here that our methodology stimulates the learning of mathematics by activating the same cognitive means by which children learn and retain stories: the ability to assimilate contextually related information. Virtually all children are competent contextual learners as demonstrated, not only by the learning of stories, but by the early mastery of their native language as well. At the core of the methodology is the awareness that mathematics is best retained by reconstruction rather than memorization. Consequently, it defines the antithesis of rote, and was created to eliminate rote learning (greatest source of remediation) from mathematics education forever.

Traditional paradigms in mathematics education suggest that the source of students' competence in this subject matter is a special "giftedness."

Our program presents a paradigm shift to the degree that:

1. at the foundation of the methodology is the understanding that the real gift for learning mathematics is the same one we used so successfully to learn language and stories before going to school (hence all learners are gifted by our Creator with the capacity to learn mathematics);

2. the methodology makes it very difficult for children to avoid learning mathematics, in contrast to the common notion that it is difficult for them to learn it;

3. accelerated development (by virtually all learners) is the inevitable outcome when the same pre-school competence for learning language and stories is activated for the learning of mathematics; and

4. accelerated learning, as achieved through the activation of the competent contextual learner in virtually all human beings, is a very enjoyable experience, in contrast to the "pushing" children experience when acceleration is attempted via traditional methodologies.

The application of the methodology to the teaching of primary and elementary mathematics is presented in Books I, Book II, and III: *Mathematics Power Learning for Children*.

If you are a parent or teacher, we believe you will be very surprised at the extent to which arithmetic has been presented as a sequential, developmental flow of related information in these books. Even if you can do arithmetic well, you may not have realized that it could actually make sense. As you read, you will experience the contextually related flow of concepts and skills in your mind. Consequently, your learning of the mathematics will become as certain as the learning of a story. You will discover that you can, simultaneously, learn the subject matter in these books and learn how to teach it to your children, if you are a parent; or to your students, if you are a teacher. You will now be able to provide meaningful explanations to those whose mathematical development you are in a position to influence.

It was by means of this methodology that so many "math-anxious" elementary teachers, over the years, learned the subject matter of arithmetic and Algebra I simultaneously as they learned to teach it. In fact, the vast majority of them now enjoy teaching mathematics due to their surprise discovery of its meanings. The strength of our statistical analyses provides effective testimony to the success of their efforts, and to the power of this methodology in the teaching and learning of mathematics.

We are confident that the pedagogical strategies and techniques in our three books represent a very significant breakthrough in mathematics education.

Everard Barrett

THE UNISON RESPONSE ACTIVITY

Frequently throughout our three texts, we request that you engage learners in **vocal**, rapid response, unisonous activities. The purpose of these activities is to speed up some cognitive way of knowing, which is the foundation upon which a considerable amount of knowledge is built.

One of your most important objectives, as you move learners through our "focus and concentration" activities, is a **strong, confident, unison response**.

When this happens, it is time to challenge **some individuals** (particularly the most reluctant participants) to answer by themselves, as you move them through four or five questions.

Be sure that no learner even attempts to help any individual you call on.

After achieving the confident unison responses, it is quite appropriate to vary between group and individual participation.

Learners will begin to understand that "unison time" is when they must "get ready," since they are expecting you to check on them individually.

While you are engaging them in the "rapid-fire" exercises, **keep your eyes fixed on the learners** to ensure that
> 1. they are **all** staring at the chart (or blackboard).
> 2. they are **all** responding.

The rapid-response exercises are to be moved along as quickly as the learners' responses will permit. Neither move so quickly as to overwhelm them, nor so slowly as to bore them. Find the right pace.

Speed makes it a game in which you can challenge them with, "Let's see who will win, you or me?" or "Let's see if I can catch you."

On the many occasions you will be engaging learners in the rapid-response exercises, you are to **"cut" the activity at the peak of excitement**. You will find them highly motivated to resume the challenge on subsequent days.

Throughout our twenty years of intense and sustained "hands on" staff development interventions, we have confirmed, over and over again, the power of this strategy. Your requirement that **every learner** must simultaneously vocalize the response, virtually guarantees that each participant will carefully monitor himself or herself, since no one wants his or her voice to say the wrong answer. Vocalizing in unison also permits insecure learners to respond softly, when they are unsure, and strongly, when they are confident. This encourages the most reluctant learners to participate. In addition, the need to respond rapidly induces an extraordinary level of focus and concentration among learners. This intense degree of concentration is experienced by learners as a game. Many observers over the years will attest to this reality. The social dimension of this activity permits learners to experience and enjoy an intense sense of participation (with their peers), in which they are attempting to defeat the teacher who has declared his or her intention to "beat" or "catch" them. Finally, the reluctant learners' expectation that they will be called on to respond to questions on a daily basis will keep them focussed at all times.

Traditional educational practice has generally failed to engage certain types of personalities among learners. Shy, introverted, as well as socially and physically aggressive individuals are, all too often, among the poorest performers in traditional mathematics education classroom strategies. Through the years, however, teachers everywhere have told us (and our data substantiates their claims) that our unison response activities have brought them unprecedented success in engaging the effective participation of the traditionally reluctant learner. This, in turn, has led to a vast improvement of the performance of such students in traditional educational circumstances.

We are convinced, therefore, that these (and many others within our three texts) are pedagogical means whereby the intellects of such individuals can be engaged with respect to their academic objectives, and their capacity for leadership harnessed for the purpose of teaching mathematics to small groups of slow learners. If this is exercised as a deliberate aspect of educational practice, with adequate counseling and training, such individuals will become very able and effective assistants to their teachers. They will acquire a strong sense of self-esteem, self-confidence, self-assurance, and responsibility for the learning of their peers. The youngsters who practice social responsibility in school are likely to be socially responsible adults.

Consider the powerful impact that this phenomenon would make on the prevailing attitudes toward the learning of mathematics. Peer pressure would certainly be transformed from negative to positive, by the very group of individuals who determine what form it should take.

COUNTING NUMBERS

Objective: The learners will count twos, threes, fours, fives, sixes, sevens, eights, nines, and tens.

Place a box with many bundles of sticks in front of the learners.

Each bundle should contain from one to four sticks.

There should be ten ones; ten bundles of two; ten bundles of three; and ten bundles of four.

Mix them up in the box.

Ask learners to pick out as many bundles of two as they can, and count them simultaneously: "one two," "two twos," "three twos, " "four twos," and so on, up to "ten twos."

Return the bundles of two to the box and mix them up with the others.

Ask learners to pick out as many bundles of four as they can, and count them simultaneously: "one four," "two fours," "three fours, " "four fours," and so on, up to "ten fours."

Similarly, have learners count the bundles of three after returning the bundles of four to the box, and mixing them up with the others.

Finally, have learners count the "bundles of one" after returning the bundles of three to the box and mixing them up with the others.

Place a box containing bundles of five, seven, and nine sticks each, in front of the learners. Mix them up.

Ask learners to pick out as many bundles of five as they can, and count them simultaneously: "one five," "two fives," "three fives, " "four fives," and so on, up to "ten fives."

Similarly, have learners count the bundles of seven, after returning the bundles of five to the box, and mixing them up with the others.

Finally, have learners count the bundles of nine after returning the bundles of seven to the box, and mixing them up with the others.

Repeat the above activity with ten bundles of each of six, eight, and ten sticks.

Have the learners apply the concepts of this section to the problems provided below.

Ask the learners, "If you pay $3 for one pen, how would you find out how much to pay for two pens?"

Learners are likely to suggest adding $3 to $3.

Learners conclude that two pens cost $6.

Ask, "If you pay $3 for one pen, how would you find out how much to pay for three pens?"

Learners are likely to suggest the following addition: $3 + $3 + $3.

Learners conclude that three pens cost $9.

Ask, "If you pay $3 for one pen, how would you find out how much to pay for four pens?"

Learners are likely to suggest the following addition: $3 + $3 + $3 +$3.

Learners conclude that four pens cost $12.

Ask, "If one ball costs $7, how much would you pay for six of those balls?"

Allow learners to add and conclude that the cost of six balls is $42.

Ask, "If one radio costs $48, how much would four radios cost?"

Allow learners to add and conclude that the cost of four radios is $192.

Ask, "If a TV set costs $497, how much would six sets cost?"

Allow learners to add and conclude that the cost of six TV Sets is $2,982.

Have learners practice the examples of Facility Exercises #1 (Workbook II) to the level of facility; **then move on**.

MASTERING THE MULTIPLICATION FACTS QUICKLY

Objective: The learner will acquire instant and accurate recall of all multiplication facts.

Teaching the "two-times" and "one-time" multiplication facts

Write the following on the board:

1+1	2+2	3+3	4+4	5+5	6+6	7+7	8+8	9+9	10+10
2 x 1	2 x 2	2 x 3	2 x 4	2 x 5	2 x 6	2 x 7	2 x 8	2 x 9	2 x 10

Tell the learners to respond rapidly when you tap the additions in the top row.

Vary the sequence through which you tap them.

After all learners have demonstrated their facility at responding instantly and accurately to the additions, you must have them learn to read expressions in the second row.

Point out, for example, that 2x5 says, "two fives" or "two times five."

Now ask, "What does 2x7 say?" (Two sevens or two times seven)

Keep pointing to the expressions in the second row and asking what each one says.

Be sure the learners can read each expression in the second row both ways.

At this point, you must show learners the link between expressions in the second row, and corresponding expressions in the first.

For example, have learners understand that "two sevens" or "two times seven" means "seven plus seven."

Now ask, "What does two times nine mean?"

Be sure that learners can explain what each expression in the second row means.

Have learners understand that in the same way Bill is a different name for the person called William, "two times six" is a different name for the number called "six plus six."

Write the following on the board:

$$2x1 = 1+1 \qquad 2x3 = 3+3 \qquad 2x5 = 5+5 \qquad 2x7 = 7+7 \qquad 2x9 = 9+9$$
$$2x2 = 2+2 \qquad 2x4 = 4+4 \qquad 2x6 = 6+6 \qquad 2x8 = 8+8 \qquad 2x10 = 10+10$$

Tell learners that it is the equal sign between 2x4 and 4+4, for example, which tells us that even though they both sound and look different, they are names for the same number.

You must also explain by saying that, for example, two times nine **means** nine plus nine.

Now return to the first expressions you wrote on the board.

Tell learners, "Anyone who knows eight plus eight knows two times eight."

Ask,
"What is 8+8?"
"So what is 2x8?"

"What is 3+3?"
"So what is 2x3?"

"What is 5+5?"
"So what is 2x5?"

Continue to ask similar questions until learners respond with facility.

At this point tell learners, "If I ask you for the answer to 2x7, you must quickly think of 7+7, and immediately answer, 'Fourteen.'"

Practice in different ways:

1. **Auditory stimulus, auditory response**
   For example, you ask, "Two sixes?" or "Two times six?" and learners respond, "Twelve."

   Be sure to ask the questions both ways.

2. **Visual stimulus, auditory response**
   Have the learners respond correctly as you rapidly tap the expressions in the second row.

   Vary the sequence through which you tap them.

You must now have learners see, for example, that 2x6 and 6x2 are two different names for the same number.

Explain to them that we get 2x6 or two sixes by counting sixes; so 2x6 represents

2 bundles of 6 sticks each.

Similarly, we get 6x2 or six twos by counting twos; so 6x2 represents 6 bundles of 2 sticks each.

Learners can check to see that 2 bundles of 6 sticks each are the same quantity as 6 bundles of 2 sticks each.

This is why we can write 2x6 = 6x2.

Learners can similarly check to see that 2x9 = 9x2; that 2x4 = 4x2; and so on.

On the **Professor B Times Tables Chart**, the expressions 2x1, 2x2, 2x3, 2x4, and so on, up to 2x10, appear on the second row; whereas 1x2, 2x2, 3x2, 4x2, and so on, up to 10x2, appear on the second column.

For five consecutive lessons, you should rapidly tap various expressions on the second row, and second column, while learners respond rapidly and accurately.

If you are tapping rapidly enough (about 40 responses per minute), you need not conduct this exercise for more than five minutes per lesson.

For each of the last three lessons that you are tapping the two-times facts on the chart, be sure learners also participate in the activities below:

1. Call on many individuals (particularly the slowest) to answer (one at a time) four or five rapid questions on the two-times multiplication facts.
2. Call on learners (one at a time) to say the multiples of two up to twenty (after the group has recited them in unison two times). Be sure they receive no help from anyone while they are reciting the multiples.
3. Call on learners (one at a time) to say the multiples of two backward from twenty to two.
4. Stand in front of the learners and pick up a number of bundles of two sticks each (five bundles, for example). Ask, "How many bundles?" (Five) "How many sticks?" (Ten) Continue to pick up different numbers of bundles and ask the same two questions (for each set of bundles).
5. Call on many individuals (particularly the slowest) to answer four or five division questions such as, "How many twos are in twelve?" (Six)

By the fourth day of tapping on the two-times multiplication facts, you can introduce the one-times multiplication facts.

Explain that 1x7, for example, represents one bundle of seven sticks.

You may demonstrate this by wrapping an elastic band around seven sticks.

Have them see that one bundle of 7 sticks equals seven sticks (take off the elastic band and count seven sticks).

So 1x7 equals 7.

Similarly, demonstrate 1x3 equals 3, 1x6 equals 6, and so on.

Explain that 4x1, for example, represents four bundles of one stick each.

You may demonstrate one bundle of one stick by wrapping an elastic band around one stick.

So 4x1 represents four such bundles.

Clearly, if we remove the elastic bands from each of these four "one-stick" bundles, there will be just four sticks.

So 4x1 equals 4.

Have learners conclude that 4x1 = 1x4 since, in either case, we get four sticks.

Similarly demonstrate that 2x1 = 1x2 = 2, 3x1 = 1x3 = 3, and so on, up to 10x1 = 1x10 = 10.

On the **Professor B Times Tables Chart**, the expressions 1x1, 1x2, 1x3, 1x4, and so on, up to 1x10, appear on the first row; whereas 1x1, 2x1, 3x1, 4x1, and so on, up to 10x1, appear on the first column.

Consequently, on the fourth and fifth days, you should be randomly tapping expressions within the first two rows and first two columns, while learners respond rapidly and accurately.

Having attained mastery of the two-times multiplication facts, it will be sustained by means of
   1. daily tapping on the **Professor B Times Tables Chart;** and
   2. multiplication of ten-digit numbers by 2 (see below).

By having learners multiply ten-digit numbers by two, they will begin to acquire the skill of multiplication, while also reinforcing their knowledge of the (two-times) facts.

At this point, we will not have learners refer to place value as they do multiplication examples.

It is sufficient, for now, that they concentrate on the skill of multiplying a large number by two.

Write on the board:

$$\begin{array}{r} 123,456,789 \\ \underline{\text{x2}} \end{array}$$

Have learners copy this example.

Tell learners, "Say what I touch."

Starting on the right of the example above, touch the 2, the times sign, and the 9.

Have learners say, "Two times 9."

Ask, "Two times 9 equals _____?"

Tell learners, "Put the 8 under the 9 and write the 'one' on top of the 8."

Have learners write down the 8 and carry the one on their own sheets.

Touch the 2, the times sign, and the 8.

Have learners say, "Two times 8."

Ask, "Two times 8 equals _____?"

Tell learners, "Add the 'little one,' on top of the 8, to the 16."

Ask,
    "Sixteen plus one equals _____?"
    "Where do we write the 7?"
    "Where do we write the one?"

Have learners write the 7 under the 8 and the little one on top of the 7.

Touch the 2, the times sign, and the 7.

Learners say, "Two times 7."

Ask,
    "Two times 7 equals _____?"
    "What do we do now?"

Tell learners,
    "Don't ever forget to add the little one!"
    "Add the little one, on top of the 7, to the 14."

Ask,
    "Fourteen plus one equals _____?"
    "What do we do now?"

Have learners write the 5 under the 7, and the little one on top of the 6.

Touch the 2, the times sign, and the 6.

Learners say, "Two times 6."

Ask,
    "Two times 6 equals _____?"
    "What do we do now?"
    "Will you ever forget the little one?"
    "Twelve plus one equals _____?"
    "What do we do now?"
    "Are you going to do this by yourselves, or are you waiting for me to do it
    for you?"

Have learners write the 3 under the 6, and the little one on top of the 5 **before** you write it on the board.

From this point forward, be sure learners do the writing at each step on their own example, before you write it on the board.

Similarly lead learners through the "two times five" step; then the "two times four" step.

After learners have written the 9 under the 4, ask, "Is there a little one to carry?"

Similarly, lead learners through the "two times three" step.

After learners have said, "Two times 3 equals 6," ask, "Is there a little one to add to the 6?"

Similarly, elicit the rest of the example.

The work will look like this:

```
    11 1 1 1
 123,456,789
          x2
 246,913,578
```

Now write on the board:

```
  123,456,789
+ 123,456,789
```

Have learners copy this example from the board and do it.

Be sure they notice that this addition example has the same answer as the previous multiplication example.

Write the following on the board:

```
 392,857,416
         x2
```

Lead learners through this example in the same manner as above.

Write on the board:

```
  392,857,416
+ 392,857,416
```

Have learners copy this example and do it.

Is the answer the same as the previous multiplication example?

Our objective, at this point, is to have learners develop the capacity to do long multiplications, by themselves, with a minimum of mistakes.

Remember that once the learner is diagnosed as having the know-how, an excessive number of wrong answers merely provides objective feedback, which informs us that more practice is necessary.

The introduction of learners to long multiplications must be done with great care.

Do not (at this point) give them an example and tell them to do it by themselves.

Proceed as follows:
1. Write another example (similar to the one above) on the board and have learners copy it.
2. On this example, tell learners to do the first step by themselves.
3. Walk around the room, check the learners' work, and ascertain the types of errors they tend to make.
4. Do the work on the board, while commenting on their errors.
5. Tell them to do the second step by themselves.
6. Repeat steps 3 and 4.
7. Continue doing **one step** at a time followed by #3 and #4.

Follow this "one-step-at-a-time" procedure on a **daily basis,** until learners have facility with it.

After learners have acquired facility with one-step-at-a-time, we proceed as follows:
1. Write another example (similar to the one above) on the board and have learners copy it.
2. On this example, tell learners to do the **first two** steps by themselves.
3. Walk around the room, check the learners' work, and ascertain the types of errors they tend to make.
4. Do the work on the board, while commenting on their errors.
5. Tell them to do the next two steps by themselves.
6. Repeat steps 3 and 4.
7. Continue doing **two steps** at a time followed by #3 and #4.

Follow this "two-steps-at-a-time" procedure on a **daily basis,** until learners have facility with it.

After learners have acquired facility with two-steps-at-a-time, you must have them develop facility with "three-steps-at-a-time," then "four-steps-at-a-time," and so on.

The examples in the next set of facility exercises are provided for carrying out the above procedures.

Have learners practice the examples of Facility Exercises #2 and #3 (Workbook II) to the level of facility; **then move on.**

Teaching the three-times multiplication facts

Be sure that over the next two or three days, as you go through Phases I, II, and III (each day), you continue to tap the first two columns and rows in order to maintain learners' mastery of the one-times and two-times multiplication facts.

A very effective technique for teaching the three-times multiplication facts is described in this section.

Phases I, II, and III, described below, should be completed in about 30 minutes.

Learners should be led through all three for each of three consecutive lessons.

Phase I

Prepare ten bundles of three sticks each.

Secure each with an elastic band.

Place them side by side in front of the learners.

From this point forward, the rest of Phase I should take about twenty minutes.

Hold up both of your hands, palms about two inches apart, and facing the learners.

Extend your right "little finger" and fold all the others.

Tell the learners to pretend the little finger is the first bundle of three on their left.

Have them say, "Three."

Now unfold the finger right next to the extended little finger (the right ring finger).

As you unfold it, say, "And three more coming up."

This represents the second bundle of three.

Tell them, "Three and three more are six. Say six."

For the next ten seconds, you must "flick" one of the following two possibilities on the right hand:
1. the little finger; or,
2. the little finger and the ring finger **(both extended at the same time)**.

As you alternatively flick these two possibilities, the learners will respond, "Three, six, three, six, three, six," and so on.

It is very important that all learners are responding in a strong, confident, unison response.

Now unfold the finger right next to the ring finger on the right hand (the middle finger).

As you unfold it say, "And three more coming up."

This represents the third bundle of three.

Tell them, "Six and three more are nine. Say nine."

As you do this, be sure that the three fingers are extended: the little finger, the ring finger, and the middle finger.

For the next minute, you must rapidly flick different examples from among the following three possibilities on the right hand, in a random sequence:
1. the little finger;
2. the little finger and the ring finger **(both extended at the same time)**;
3. the little finger, the ring finger, and the middle finger **(all three extended at the same time)**.

As you flick these three possibilities, the learners should not be able to predict which one is coming up next.

You must always be trying to "catch" them.

Typically, they will rapidly respond, "Six", for a showing of the two fingers; "Nine," for a showing of the three fingers; "Three," for a showing of the one; and so on.

After you achieve a strong, confident, unison response, stop the activity and request that each of the slowest learners makes four or five responses **(absolutely no help from anyone)** as you flick fingers appropriately.

Now unfold the finger right next to the middle finger on the right hand (the fore finger).

As you unfold it say, "And three more coming up."

This represents the fourth bundle of three.

Tell them, "Nine and three more are twelve. Say twelve."

As you do this, be sure that all four fingers are extended.

Randomly flick among the first four fingers.

An example follows:
1. Flick the first three. Learners respond, "Nine."
2. Flick the first one. Learners respond, "Three."
3. Flick the first four. Learners respond, "Twelve."
4. Flick the first three. Learners respond, "Nine."
5. Flick the first two. Learners respond, "Six."
6. Flick the first three. Learners respond, "Nine."
7. Flick the first four. Learners respond, "Twelve."
8. Flick the first one. Learners respond, "Three."

This random sequence continues for one to two minutes.

Remember to stop the strong, confident, unison response (a few times) and check on the slowest individuals (if they do not seem to be responding with the group).

Have each one of them make four or five responses (absolutely no help from anyone).

Continue similarly until you get to ten fingers (ten bundles of three).

Facility with ten fingers means that if you flick any set of fingers, the first eight, for example, learners will immediately respond, "Twenty-four."

Please be reminded that when you flick a set of ten, nine, eight, seven, six, five, four, three, or two fingers they must be the **first ten, nine, eight, seven, six, five, four, three, or two from the right**.

Practice for five minutes to the level of facility; **then move on** to Phase II.

Phase II

Now flick a set of fingers, the first six, for example, and say, "Six threes."

Have learners respond, "Eighteen."

If you flick five fingers (the first five from the right) say, "Five threes."

Learners respond, "Fifteen."

Flick nine fingers (the first nine from the right) and say, "Nine threes."

Learners respond, "Twenty-seven."

Every time you flick a set of fingers in Phase II, you say, "Eight threes," or "Four threes," or "Seven threes" according to how many fingers are extended.

The learners answer each time.

Practice the above for five minutes to the level of facility; **then move on** to Phase III.

Phase III

Phase III should take about five minutes.

Place both hands behind your back.

Now only use your voice and ask questions which learners are to answer, **without the use of fingers**: "Five threes?", "Eight threes?", "Two threes?", "Four threes?", "Seven threes?"; and so on.

Continue asking learners many questions until facility is achieved.

With proper application of this method, it takes less than 30 minutes for learners to know the three times multiplication facts.

At this point, you may call on many individual learners, particularly the slowest, (be absolutely certain that they receive help from no one) and ask each one

1. four or five questions on the three times multiplication facts (such as, "Six threes?", "Nine threes?"; and so on);
2. to say the multiples of three forward from three to thirty;
3. to say the multiples of three backward from thirty to three;
4. four or five questions on the associated division facts (such as, "How many threes are in fifteen?", "How many threes in twenty-seven?"); and
5. to pick up a number of bundles (let's say, six bundles) and answer two questions: "How many bundles?" and "How many sticks?"

Continue asking learners the above types of questions until facility is achieved; **then move on**.

Having attained mastery of the three times multiplication facts over two or three lessons (go through Phases I, II, and III during each lesson), it will be sustained by means of

1. daily tapping of the **Professor B Times Tables Chart;** and
2. multiplication of ten-digit numbers by 3.

By the finger technique for teaching these multiplication facts, a showing of the first seven fingers represents seven bundles of three each, or seven threes.

The symbolic representation for seven threes is 7x3.

Similarly, a showing of the first four fingers represents four bundles of three each, or four threes.

The symbolic representation for four threes is 4x3.

These symbolic representations, 1x3, 2x3, 3x3, 4x3, and so on, up to 10x3 appear as the third column on the **Professor B Times Tables Chart**.

By reversing each one of these, we get 3x1, 3x2, 3x3, 3x4, and so on, up to 3x10.

These symbolic representations appear as the third row of the **Professor B Times Tables Chart**.

Be sure learners understand, for example, that 8x3 = 3x8.

Explain this by demonstrating that 8 bundles, of 3 sticks each, are the same quantity (of sticks) as 3 bundles, of 8 sticks each.

Similarly, have learners understand the other equivalences between the third column and the third row.

After you have shown how the third column symbolizes the three times multiplication facts, as demonstrated on your fingers, and you have shown the equivalences linking column three to row three, you must first begin to tap the symbolic representations on the third column, while they (the learners) respond rapidly and accurately. Do this for about one minute.

Immediately after, begin tapping on the third row (while learners respond) for another minute.

For the next three minutes, tap randomly within the first three rows and the first three columns.

Thereafter, you must tap the first three columns and first three rows five minutes per day for four consecutive lessons.

During the same five lessons that you tap the first three columns and rows, you should use the strategies above (for developing learners' skill in multiplying ten-digit numbers by two) to have the learners become skilled at multiplying ten-digit numbers by three.

Elicit from learners that multiplying a number by three is a short-cut for the repeated addition of that number.

They will strengthen multiplication skills, while also reinforcing the three-times multiplication facts.

Please note that class work and homework assignments should contain a mixture of multiplications (of ten-digit numbers) by two and three.

Following these five days of tapping and doing "long multiplication" (as a means of strengthening the two- and three-times multiplication facts), you must immediately begin to teach the four-times multiplication facts.

Have learners practice the examples of Facility Exercises #4 and #5 (Workbook II) to the level of facility; **then move on**.

Teaching the four-times multiplication facts

Be sure that, over the next two to three days, as you go through Phases I, II, and III (each day), you continue to tap the first three columns and rows, in order to maintain learners' mastery of previously learned multiplication facts.

After placing ten bundles of four sticks each in front of the learners, apply Phases I, II, and III to bundles of four (instead of three).

Application of Phases I, II, and III to each finger representing a bundle of four will lead, after two to three lessons (Phases I, II, and III are completed in each lesson), to learners' mastery of the four-times multiplication facts.

Mastery, once attained, will be sustained by means of
1. **daily** tapping on the **Professor B Times Tables Chart;** and
2. multiplication of ten-digit numbers by 4.

After you have shown how the fourth column (on the chart) symbolizes the four-times multiplication facts as demonstrated on your fingers, and you have shown the equivalences linking column four to row four, you must begin to tap the symbolic representations on the fourth column, while the learners respond rapidly and accurately.

Do this for one minute.

Immediately after, begin tapping on the fourth row (while learners respond) for another minute. For the next three minutes, tap randomly within the first four rows and columns.

Thereafter, you must tap the first four columns and rows five minutes per day for four consecutive lessons.

During the same five lessons that you tap the first four columns and rows, you should use the same strategies above (for developing learners' skills in multiplying ten-digit numbers by two and three) to have the learners become skilled at multiplying ten-digit numbers by four.

Elicit from learners that multiplying a number by four is a short-cut for the repeated addition of that number.

They will strengthen multiplication skills, while also reinforcing the four times multiplication facts.

Please note that class work and homework assignments should contain a mixture of multiplications (of ten-digit numbers) by two, three, and four.

Following these five days of tapping and doing long multiplications, you must immediately begin to teach the five times multiplication facts.

Have learners practice the examples of Facility Exercises #6 and #7 (Workbook II) to the level of facility; **then move on**.

Facility Exercises #8 are the first of nine "Mixed Practice" experiences for the learners in Workbook II.

Teaching the five-times multiplication facts

Be sure that, over the next two to three days, as you go through Phases I, II, and III (each day), you continue to tap within the first four columns and rows.

Proceed to replicate all the same strategies and techniques for teaching the four-times facts, for the teaching of the five-times facts.

After two or three lessons spent on Phases I, II, and III, you must begin tapping the first five columns and rows.

Continue this for four consecutive lessons (five minutes per day).

During the same five lessons that you tap the first five columns and rows, have the learners practice the multiplication of ten-digit numbers by five.

Elicit from learners that multiplying a number by five is a short-cut for the repeated addition of that number.

Class work and homework should contain a mixture of multiplications (of ten-digit numbers) by two, three, four, and five.

Following these five days of tapping and doing long multiplications, you must immediately begin to teach the six-times multiplication facts.

Have learners practice the examples of Facility Exercises #9 and #10 (Workbook II) to the level of facility; **then move on**.

Teaching the six-times multiplication facts

Be sure that, over the next two to three days, as you go through Phases I, II, and III (each day), you continue to tap within the first five columns and rows.

Proceed to replicate all the same strategies and techniques for teaching the five-times facts, for the teaching of the six-times facts.

After two or three lessons spent on Phases I, II, and III, you must begin tapping the first six columns and rows.

Continue this for four consecutive lessons (five minutes per day).

During the same five lessons that you tap the first six columns and rows, have the learners practice the multiplication of ten-digit numbers by six.

Elicit from learners that multiplying a number by six is a short-cut for the repeated addition of that number.

Class work and homework should contain a mixture of long multiplications by two, three, four, five, and six.

Following these five days of tapping and doing long multiplications, you must immediately begin to teach the seven times multiplication facts.

Have learners practice the examples of Facility Exercises #11 and #12 (Workbook II) to the level of facility; **then move on**.

Teaching the seven-times multiplication facts

Be sure that, over the next two to three days, as you go through Phases I, II, and III (each day), you continue to tap within the first six columns and rows.

Proceed to replicate all the same strategies and techniques for teaching the six-times facts, for the teaching of the seven-times facts.

After two or three lessons spent on Phases I, II, and III, you must begin tapping the first seven columns and rows.

Continue this for four consecutive lessons (five minutes per day).

During the same five lessons that you tap the first seven columns and rows, have the learners practice the multiplication of ten-digit numbers by seven.

Elicit from learners that multiplying a number by seven is a short-cut for the repeated addition of that number.

Class work and homework should contain a mixture of long multiplications by two, three, four, five, six, and seven.

Following these five days of tapping and doing long multiplications, you must immediately begin to teach the eight-times multiplication facts.

Have learners practice the examples of Facility Exercises #13 and #14 (Workbook II) to the level of facility; **then move on**.

Teaching the eight-times multiplication facts

Be sure that, over the next two to three days, as you go through Phases I, II, and III (each day), you continue to tap within the first seven columns and rows.

Proceed to replicate all the same strategies and techniques for teaching the seven-times facts, for the teaching of the eight-times facts.

After two or three lessons spent on Phases I, II, and III, you must begin tapping the first eight columns and rows.

Continue this for four consecutive lessons (five minutes per day).

During the same five lessons that you tap the first eight columns and rows, have the learners practice the multiplication of ten-digit numbers by eight.

Elicit from learners that multiplying a number by eight is a short-cut for the repeated addition of that number.

Class work and homework should contain a mixture of long multiplications by two, three, four, five, six, seven, and eight.

Following these five days of tapping and doing long multiplications, you must immediately begin to teach the nine-times multiplication facts.

Have learners practice the examples of Facility Exercises #15 and #16 (Workbook II) to the level of facility; **then move on**.

Teaching the nine-times multiplication facts

Be sure that, over the next two to three days, as you go through Phases I, II, and III (each day), you continue to tap within the first eight columns and rows.

Proceed to replicate all the same strategies and techniques for teaching the eight-times facts, for the teaching of the nine-times facts.

After two or three lessons spent on Phases I, II, and III, you must begin tapping the first nine columns and rows.

Continue this for four consecutive lessons (five minutes per day).

During the same five lessons that you tap the first nine columns and rows, have the learners practice the multiplication of ten-digit numbers by nine.

Elicit from learners that multiplying a number by nine is a short-cut for the repeated addition of that number.

Class work and homework should contain a mixture of long multiplications by two, three, four, five, six, seven, eight, and nine.

Following these five days of tapping and doing long multiplications by nine (or less), you must immediately begin to teach the ten-times multiplication facts.

We now describe an alternate method for knowing the nine-times multiplication facts.

Have learners hold up their hands with all fingers extended; palms toward their faces.

Direct learners as follows:

"Call your left thumb number one; the next finger, number two; the next, number three; the next, number four; the next, number five; the next, number six; the next, number seven; the next, number eight; the next, number nine; and the right thumb, number ten."

"Nine times seven."
"What was the last numeral you heard?" (Seven)
"Fold finger number seven and look at your hands."
"How many fingers are on the left of the folded finger?" (Six)
"How many fingers are on the right of the folded finger?" (Three)
"So, nine times seven?" (Sixty-three)

"Nine times three."
"What was the last numeral you heard?" (Three)
"Fold finger number three and look at your hands."
"How many fingers are on the left of the folded finger?" (Two)
"How many fingers are on the right of the folded finger?" (Seven)

"So, nine times three?"

The remaining nine-times multiplication facts can be similarly recalled.

Have learners practice the above finger process to the level of facility.

Have learners practice the examples of Facility Exercises #17 and #18 (Workbook II) to the level of facility; **then move on**.

Teaching the ten-times multiplication facts

Be sure that, over the next two to three days, as you go through Phases I, II, and III (each day), you continue to tap within the first nine columns and rows.

Proceed to replicate all the same strategies and techniques for teaching the nine-times facts, for the teaching of the ten-times facts.

After two or three lessons spent on Phases I, II, and III, you must begin tapping the first ten columns and rows.

Continue this for two consecutive lessons (five minutes per day).

During the same three lessons that you tap all ten columns and rows, have the learners continue practicing (during class work and homework) the multiplication of large numbers, by two through nine.

Facility Exercises #19 through #21 (Workbook II) provide mixed practice for the learners.

LINKING MULTIPLICATION AND DIVISION FACTS

Objectives: 1. Given a multiplication fact, the learner will give the answer to the related division fact(s).
2. Given an equation consisting of a product of two whole numbers equal to a third, and assuming
   (a) the products involved are chosen from the set of multiplication facts, and
   (b) one of the factors is missing,
   the learner will find the missing factor.
3. The learner will respond, quickly and accurately, to "short division" questions in which the divisor, quotient, and dividend involve a multiplication fact.

Tell learners, "Listen very carefully to what I ask, and you will hear the answer in the question itself."

Ask the following questions:
   "Two fives equal ten; so how many fives are in ten?" (Two)
   "Five threes equal fifteen; so how many threes are in fifteen?" (Five)
   "Four sevens equal twenty-eight; so how many sevens are in twenty-eight?" (Four)
   "Six nines equal fifty-four; so how many nines are in fifty-four?"
   "Seven eights equal fifty-six; so how many eights are in fifty-six?"
   "Eight times three equal twenty-four; so how many threes are in twenty-four?"
   "Three times six equal eighteen; so how many sixes are in eighteen?"

We now ask the above questions symbolically.

Write the following on the board:

$2 \times 7 = 14$; so, $7 \overline{)14}$

$3 \times 5 = 15$; so, $5 \overline{)15}$

$7 \times 6 = 42$; so, $6 \overline{)42}$

Be sure learners see, for example, that "2x7=14; so, $7\overline{)14}$ " asks the question, "Two sevens equal fourteen; so how many sevens are in fourteen?"

Have them answer the other two questions on the board.

Have learners practice the examples in Facility Exercises #22 (Workbook II) to the level of facility; **then move on.**

Have learners look at 3x ____ =12, for example, and ask the question, "Three times what equals twelve?" before writing the answer.

Have learners look at ____ x 4=20, for example, and ask the question, "What times four equals twenty?" before writing the answer.

While doing the examples of Facility Exercises #23 (Workbook II), have learners ask the appropriate questions before writing answers.

Have learners practice the examples of Facility Exercises #23 to the level of facility; **then move on.**

Write the questions below on the board:
Three times what equals twelve?
How many threes are in twelve?

Ask,
"What is the answer to the first question?" (Four)
"What is the answer to the second question?" (Four)

Be sure learners see that both questions have the same answer.

Write the questions below on the board:
Four times what equals twenty?
How many fours are in twenty?

Ask, "Do both questions have the same answer?"

Write the following on the board:

$5\overline{)35}$

Ask, "What question does this ask?" (As a consequence of previous work, learners should answer, "How many fives are in thirty-five?")

Tell learners we can find the answer to $5\overline{)35}$ by asking, "Five times what equals thirty-five?"
This is possible, since **both questions have the same answer.**

Be sure learners see that since seven is the answer to, "Five times what equals thirty-five?", it (seven) is also the answer to $5\overline{)35}$ (How many fives are in thirty-five?).

Write the following on the board:

$3\overline{)6}$ $9\overline{)45}$ $4\overline{)12}$

$5\overline{)50}$ $7\overline{)49}$ $6\overline{)48}$

The answer to the example $5\overline{)35}$ was found by asking the question, "Five times what equals thirty-five?"

Have learners ask the questions which give the answers to each of the examples on the board.

Have learners focus on the example $6\overline{)48}$. The question which gives the answer is, "Six times what equals forty-eight?" Despite being able to ask the question, some learners may not know the answer immediately. The strategy below has proven to be very helpful.

For all division examples in the next set of Facility Exercises, proceed as demonstrated with the example $6\overline{)48}$.

Write the following on the board:

$$5$$

$$6\overline{)48}$$

Tell learners, "Always try five first."

Write 5 above the example.

Ask,
   "Six times five equals ____ ?" (Learners say, "Thirty")
   "Up or down?"

Have learners compare their answer (thirty) with the 48.

Since 48 is larger, have them say, "Up."

Now ask, "Up to what?"

Have learners answer, "Six."

Cross out the 5 on the board and write 6 next to it. See below.

$$\cancel{5}\,6$$

$$6\overline{)48}$$

Ask,

"Six times six equals ____ ?" (Learners say, "Thirty-six")
"Up or down?"

Have learners compare their answer (thirty-six) with the 48. Since 48 is larger, they should say, "Up."

Now ask, "Up to what?"

Have learners answer, "Seven."

Cross out the 6 on the board and write 7 next to it. See below.

$$\cancel{5}\,\cancel{6}\,7$$

$$6\overline{)48}$$

Ask,

"Six times seven equals ____ ?" (Learners say, "Forty-two")
"Up or down?"

Have learners compare their answer (forty-two) with the 48. Since 48 is larger, they should say, "Up."

Now ask, "Up to what?"

Have learners answer, "Eight."

Cross out the 7 on the board and write 8 next to it. See below.

$$\cancel{5}\,\cancel{6}\,\cancel{7}\,8$$

$$6\overline{)48}$$

Ask,

"Six times eight equals ____ ?" (Learners say, "Forty-eight")
"Up or down?"

Have learners compare their answer (forty-eight) with the 48.

Have them say, "Stay!"

Ask, "So how many sixes are in forty-eight?"

Finally, the board work appears as below:

$$\cancel{5}\,\cancel{6}\,\cancel{7}\,8$$

$$6\overset{8}{\overline{)48}}$$

Now have learners focus on the example $4\overline{)12}$.

Write the following on the board:

$$5$$

$$4\overline{)12}$$

Ask,
   "What will we always try first?" (5)
   "Four times five equals ____ ?"
   "Up or down?" ("Down," since 12 is less than 20)
   "Down to what?" (Four)

Cross out the 5 on the board and write 4 next to it.

Ask,
   "Four times four equals ____ ?"
   "Up or down?"
   "Down to what?"

Cross out the 4 on the board and write 3 next to it.

Ask,
   "Four times three equals ____ ?"
   "Up or down?"

Learners will decide to stay at 3, since 4x3 equals 12.

Finally, the board work appears as below:

$$\cancel{5}\,\cancel{4}\,3$$

$$4\overline{)12}^{\,3}$$

Traditionally, the learner who seeks the answer to $6\overline{)48}$ often starts thinking, "Six times one equals six; six times two equals twelve," and so on, up to "Six times eight equals forty-eight." By starting at, "Six times five," (in the "middle") we are closer to the answer.

After much practice, have learners use the process described above to answer the examples in Facility Exercises #24 (Workbook II).

Have learners practice the examples in Facility Exercises #24 to the level of facility; **then move on.**

PREPARING FOR DIVISION WITH REMAINDER

Objective: Given an equation involving one product and one sum on the left of the equal sign, and one of four numbers missing, the learners will find the answer.

Write on the board:

4x3 + 2 = _____

Tell learners,
  "Do the multiplication first; then add two."
  "What is your answer?" (14)

Tell learners,
  "Do the addition first; then multiply by four."
  "What is your answer?" (20)

Ask, "Are both answers the same?"

Tell learners that the rule is to multiply first. As a consequence of this rule, fourteen is the correct answer, and 4x3 + 2 is the name for one number and no other.

Have learners practice the examples of Facility Exercises #25 (Workbook II) to the level of facility; **then move on.**

SHORT DIVISION WITH REMAINDER

Objective: The learner will respond correctly to short division questions, in which the divisor and quotient are factors in one of the multiplication facts.

Write the following on the board:

$$2\overline{)10}$$

Ask,

"What question does this ask?" (How many twos are in ten?)
"What is the answer?" (Five)
"How many twos can we 'take out of' ten?"

By placing ten objects before them, have learners see they can take five twos out of ten.

Have learners take five twos out of ten in the following manner (explain it on the board):

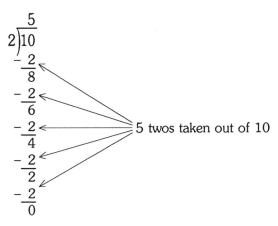

5 twos taken out of 10

After explaining the above on the board, have the learners practice this "repeated subtraction" until they can perform it, all the way through, by themselves.

Write the questions below on the board:
    How many twos are in ten?
    How many twos can we take out of ten?

Ask, "Do both questions have the same answer?"

Tell learners, "We can take five twos out of ten, because there are five twos in ten."

Have learners answer the following questions orally:
    How many threes can we take out of fifteen?
    How many fours can we take out of twenty-eight?
    How many nines can we take out of thirty-six?

Ask, "How many sevens can we take out of fifty-one?"

Lead learners to the answer of the above question by means of repeated subtraction.

Explain while showing the work on the board:

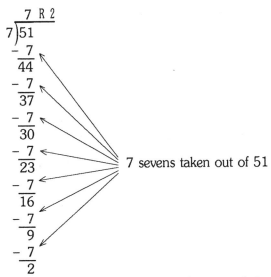

7 sevens taken out of 51

Have learners practice this repeated subtraction until they can perform it, all the way through, by themselves.

Write the following on the board:

$$5$$
$$7\overline{)51}$$

Once again, tell learners, "Always try five first."

Write 5 above the example.

Ask,
"Seven times five equals ____ ?"
"Up or down?"
"Up to what?"

Cross out the 5 on the board and write 6 next to it.

Ask,
"Seven times six equals ____ ?"
"Up or down?"
"Up to what?"

Cross out the six on the board and write 7 next to it.

Ask,
"Seven times seven equals ____ ?"
"Up or down?" (At this level of experience, many learners may say, "Up")
"Up to what?" (Many learners may say, "Eight")

Cross out the 7 and write 8 next to it.

Ask,
"Seven times eight equals ____?"
"Up or down?" (Learners will say, "Down")
"Down to what?" (Seven)
"So how many sevens can we take out of fifty-one?"
"Now after we have taken seven sevens out of fifty-one, how much is left over?"
  (Two)

Write the answer on the board as follows:

$$7\overline{)51}\text{7 R 2}$$

Have learners check as follows:

7x7+2=51

Be sure learners see that we can take 7 sevens out of 51, and 2 is left over. The answer is "seven remainder two."

You should confirm this answer by actually gathering 51 objects, and having learners make as many groups of 7 as possible.

Each example in Facility Exercises #25 (Workbook II) below is to be checked.

Here is a sample of how the learners' work will look:

	Learners' work	**Check**
Example:	$6\overline{)27}$ $\quad$ $6\overline{)27}^{\,4\,R\,3}$	6x4+3=27

Have learners practice the examples of Facility Exercises #26 to the level of facility; **then move on.**

Facility Exercises #27 are the second of nine Mixed Practice exercises for learners in Workbook II.

FOR THE APPRECIATION OF MULTIPLICATION BY LARGE NUMBERS

Objective: Learners will ask you to teach them multiplication of one large number by another.

Write on the board:

```
    1,598,762,043        1,598,762,043
             x 9         1,598,762,043
                         1,598,762,043
                         1,598,762,043
                         1,598,762,043
                         1,598,762,043
                         1,598,762,043
                         1,598,762,043
                       + 1,598,762,043
```

Have learners do both types of examples which appear on the board.

Ask, "Which one is easier?"

Point out to the learners that the large number on the board is being multiplied by the single-digit number 9.

Write on the board:

```
    43,987
   x 649
```

Have learners note that the large number 43,987 is being multiplied by the three-digit number 649.

Ask, "If we do this example by addition, how many times would we need to write the number 43,987?"

Ask, "Would you like to take a very 'lo-o-ong' time to do that addition, or would you like to learn a short-cut which would take less than six minutes?"

Tell learners that the short-cut for the repeated (even as much as six hundred forty-nine times) addition of numbers (large or small) is called the multiplication algorithm.

Emphasize that the multiplication algorithm is a short-cut.

Now ask, "Do you want to learn the multiplication algorithm?" (All learners say, "YES!")

Tell learners they will be applying the multiplication algorithm to two large numbers (as in the example on the board) in the near future.

MORE MULTIPLICATION FACTS

Objective: Learners will respond correctly to multiplication facts in which, either both factors are powers of ten, or one factor is a power of ten.

Write on the board:

2x100	3x100	4x100	5x100
6x100	7x100	8x100	9x100

Remind learners that "6x100" may be read (or renamed) as "six hundreds," just as "4x7" may be read as "four sevens."

At this point, have learners rename "5x100," for example, as "five hundreds" and write it as "500."

Ask,
"How will you rename 2x100?" (Two hundreds)
"Write it." (Learners write "200")

"How will you rename 4x100?"
"Write it." (Learners write "400")

Continue similarly for the remaining expressions above.

Write on the board:

2x1,000	3x1,000	4x1,000	5x1,000
6x1,000	7x1,000	8x1,000	9x1,000

Have learners rename "4x1,000," for example, as "four thousands" and write it as "4,000."

Ask,
"How will you rename 2x1,000?"
"Write it." (Learners write "2,000")

"How will you rename 9x1,000?"
"Write it."

Continue similarly for the remaining expressions above.

Write on the board:

2x10,000	3x10,000	4x10,000	5x10,000
6x10,000	7x10,000	8x10,000	9x10,000

Have learners rename "7x10,000," for example, as "seven ten-thousands."
Since seven tens equal seventy, then seven ten-thousands can be renamed as "seventy thousands."
This is written as "70,000."

Ask, "How will you rename 3x10,000?" (Thirty thousands)

Have them write it.

Continue similarly for the remaining expressions above.

Write on the board:

2x100,000	3x100,000	4x100,000	5x100,000
6x100,000	7x100,000	8x100,000	9x100,000

Have learners rename "8x100,000," for example, as "eight hundred-thousands" and write it as "800,000."

Ask, "How will you rename 2x100,000?"

Have them write it.

Continue similarly for the remaining expressions above.

Write on the board:

2x1,000,000	3x1,000,000	4x1,000,000	5x1,000,000
6x1,000,000	7x1,000,000	8x1,000,000	9x1,000,000

Have learners rename "2x1,000,000," for example, as "two millions" and write it as "2,000,000."

Learners must know the multiplication facts below "by heart"; both at sight, and by ear.

10x10 = 100
Ten tens equal one hundred.

10x100 = 100x10 = 1, 000
Ten hundreds equal one thousand.
One hundred tens equal one thousand.

10x1,000 = 1,000x10 = 10,000
Ten thousands equal one ten-thousand.
One thousand tens equal one ten-thousand.

10x10,000 = 10,000x10 = 100,000
Ten ten-thousands equal one hundred-thousand.
Ten thousand tens equal one hundred-thousand.

10x100,000 = 100,000x10 = 1,000,000
Ten hundred-thousands equal one million.
One hundred thousand tens equal one million.

10x1,000,000 = 1,000,000x10 = 10,000,000
Ten millions equal one ten-million.
One million tens equal one ten-million.

10x10,000,000 = 10,000,000x10 = 100,000,000
Ten ten-millions equal one hundred-million.
Ten million tens equal one hundred-million.

You should conduct many five-minute practice sessions by writing 10x10, 10x100, 10x1,000, 10x10,000, 10x100,000, 10x1,000,000, and 10x10,000,000 on the board (or on flash cards), and rapidly and randomly point to them (one at a time), as learners respond in unison with the correct answers.

You should also conduct many five-minute oral practice sessions by saying, rapidly and randomly, "Ten tens," "Ten hundreds," "Ten thousands," "Ten ten-thousands," "Ten hundred-thousands," "Ten millions," or "Ten ten-millions," (remember to vary the sequence) as learners respond with "One hundred," "One thousand," "One ten-thousand," "One hundred-thousand," "One million," "One ten-million," or "One hundred-million," respectively.

It is important for future work that all of the learners acquire quick recall of any one of the above multiplication facts.

Practice the above to the level of facility; **then move on.**

Write on the board:

2 x 3 x 5 x 7

Have the learners find the answer by first saying, "Two times three equals six"; then, "Six times five equals thirty"; and finally finding the answer by doing 30x7 on paper.

Learners conclude that 2x3x5x7=210.

Ask, "Could we find the answer another way?"

Elicit from the learners that they could start by saying, "Three times five equals fifteen"; then do 15x7 equals 105 on paper; and, finally, do 105x2 equals 210 on paper.

Learners conclude the answer is the same as before, in spite of the fact that they changed the order of the multiplications.

Ask, "Could we find the answer another way?"

Elicit from learners that they could start by saying, "Seven times three equals twenty-one"; then do 21x2 equals 42 on paper; and, finally, do 42x5 equals 210 on paper.

Once again, the answer is the same as before, in spite of the different order of the multiplications.

Elicit other ways of finding the answer from the learners.

Repeat this activity with different examples.

Write on the board:

   100 x 10

Tell learners, "Look at what happens to 100x10." (See below)

$$100 \times 10$$
$$10 \times 10 \times 10$$
$$10 \times 100$$
$$1,000$$

Tell learners, "So 100 x 10 equals 1,000."

Write on the board:

   100 x 1,000

Tell learners, "Look at what happens to 100x1,000." (See below)

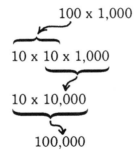

$$100 \times 1,000$$
$$10 \times 10 \times 1,000$$
$$10 \times 10,000$$
$$100,000$$

Tell learners, "So 100x1,000 equals 100,000."

Write on board:

10,000 x 1,000

Tell learners, "Look at what happens to 10,000x1,000." (See below)

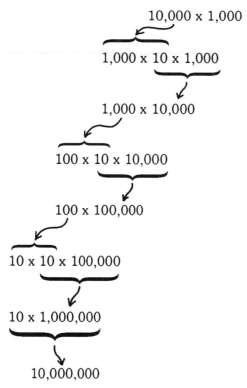

10,000 x 1,000

1,000 x 10 x 1,000

1,000 x 10,000

100 x 10 x 10,000

100 x 100,000

10 x 10 x 100,000

10 x 1,000,000

10,000,000

Tell learners, "So 10,000x1,000 equals 10,000,000."

Similarly elicit the following from the learners:

    100 x 100   = 10,000
    1,000 x 100   = 100,000
      100 x 10,000 = 1,000,000

Go back to the examples already worked out and ask the following questions:
  1. "How many zeros does the answer to 100x10 have?"
  2. "How many zeros does the answer to 100x1,000 have?"
  3. "How many zeros does the answer to 10,000x1,000 have?"
  4. "How many zeros does the answer to 100x100 have?"

5. "How many zeros does the answer to 1,000x100 have?"
6. "How many zeros does the answer to 100x10,000 have?"
7. "So how many zeros will the answer to 1,000,000x10,000 have?"

By means of the questions above, learners should discover that a quick way to find the answers to such multiplication examples is to count the zeros in the two numbers.

Practice to the level of facility; **then move on.**

Write on the board:

50 x 10

Tell learners, "Look at what happens to 50x10." (See below)

$$50 \times 10$$

5 x 10 x 10

Ask, "Do you see that 50x10 equals 5x10x10?"

Tell learners, "Look at what happens to 5x10x10." (See below)

$$5 \times 10 \times 10$$

5 x 100

Ask,
"Do you see that 5x10x10 equals 5x100?"
"Five times one hundred equals ____ ?"

Summarize the above work on the board as follows:

$$50x10 = 5x10x10$$

$$= 5x100$$

$$= 500$$

Tell learners, "So, 50x10 equals 500."

Tell learners, "Look at what happens to 10 x 50." (See below)

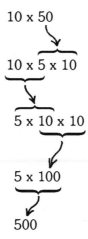

$$10 \times 50$$

$$10 \times 5 \times 10$$

$$5 \times 10 \times 10$$

$$5 \times 100$$

$$500$$

Tell learners, "So, 10 x 50 also equals 500."

As learners look at the above development, be sure they understand why "10x5" is replaced by "5x10": ten bundles of five sticks each is the same number (of sticks) as five bundles of ten each.

Ask the following questions:
 "What is 60x10? 10x30? 70x10? 10x80? 90x10? 10x10? 10x40? 20x10?"
 "Do you see a 'short-cut' for multiplying the above examples?"
 "What is your short-cut for 60x10?" (Multiply 6 by 1 and write the two zeros which you see)

Write on the board:

 50 x 100

Tell learners, "Look at what happens to 50x100." (See below)

$$50 \times 100$$

$$5 \times 10 \times 100$$

Ask, "Do you see that 50x100 equals 5x10x100?"

Tell learners, "Look at what happens to 5x10x100." (See below)

Write on the board:

$$5 \times 10 \times 100$$

$$5 \times 1,000$$

Ask,

"Do you see that 5x10x100 equals 5x1,000?"

"Five times one thousand equals ____ ?"

Summarize the above work as follows:

$$50 \times 100 = 5 \times 10 \times 100$$

$$= 5 \times 1,000$$

$$= 5,000$$

Tell learners, "So, 50x100 equals 5,000."

Tell learners, "Look at what happens to 100x50." (See below)

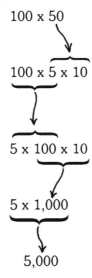

100 x 50

100 x 5 x 10

5 x 100 x 10

5 x 1,000

5,000

Tell learners, "So, 100x50 also equals 5,000."

Ask the following questions:

"What is 30x100? 100x80? 40x100? 100x70? 90x100? 100x20? 60x100? 10x100?"

"Do you see a short-cut for multiplying the above examples?"

"What is your short-cut for 30x100?"

Write on the board:

$$50 \times 1,000$$

Elicit the following from the learners (write it on the board):

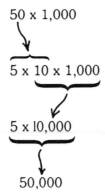

50 x 1,000

5 x 10 x 1,000

5 x 10,000

50,000

Tell learners, "So, 50x1,000 equals 50,000."

Ask, "So, what is 1,000x50?"

Ask the following questions:
"What is 70x1,000? 1,000x40? 20x1,000? 1,000x90? 30x1,000? 1,000x60? 10x1,000?"
"Do you see a short-cut for multiplying the above examples?"
"What is your short-cut for 1,000x70?"

Write on the board:

600 x 1,000

Tell learners, "Look at what happens to 600x1,000." (See below)

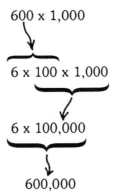

600 x 1,000

6 x 100 x 1,000

6 x 100,000

600,000

Tell learners, "So 600x1,000 equals 600,000."

Ask, "So, what is 1,000x600?"

Similarly elicit the following from the learners:
1. 3,000x10,000 = 30,000,000
2. 900,000x1,000,000 = 900,000,000,000
3. 10,000x60,000 = 600,000,000

Write on the board:

2x100 = ____   7x100 = ____
20x100 = ____   70x100 = ____
200x100 = ____   700x100 = ____

8x100 = ____   4x100 = ____
80x100 = ____   40x100 = ____
800x100 = ____   400x100 = ____

Ask the following questions:
"What is 2x100?"
"What is 20x100?"
"So, what is 200x100?"
"What is 100x200?"

"What is 7x100?"
"What is 70x100?"
"So, what is 700x100?"
"What is 100x700?"

"What is 8x100?"
"What is 80x100?"
"So, what is 800x100?"
"What is 100x800?"

"What is 4x100?"
"What is 40x100?"
"So, what is 400x100?"
"What is 100x400?"

Have learners multiply the examples of Facility Exercises #28 (Workbook II) by the method of counting zeros.

Have learners practice the examples of Facility Exercises #28 to the level of facility; **then move on.**

PREPARING FOR MULTIPLICATION
BY TWO OR MORE DIGITS

Objective: Given a product of two whole numbers, where the left factor is a two or three digit number, the learners will expand the product as a sum of two or three products.

Write on the board:

46 x 10

Forty-six tens

Have learners say the following: "Forty-six apples equal 40 apples plus 6 apples; so, 46 tens equal 40 tens plus 6 tens."

Say to learners, "Listen very carefully when I say, 'Forty-six tens.' Did you 'hear' 40 tens? Did you 'hear' 6 tens?"

Write on the board:

    46x10=40x10 + 6x10
    78x10= _____ + _____
    29x10= _____ + _____
    13x10= _____ + _____
    85x10= _____ + _____
    91x10= _____ + _____
    18x10= _____ + _____
    52x10= _____ + _____
    14x10= _____ + _____

Have individual learners go to the board, say the proper statement, and fill in the spaces appropriately. The "proper statement" for 78x10, for example, is "seventy-eight tens equal 70 tens plus 8 tens."

Write on the board:

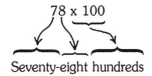

Seventy-eight hundreds

Have learners say the following, while listening very carefully to their own voices: "Seventy-eight hundreds equal 70 hundreds plus 8 hundreds."

Ask,

"Did you hear 70 hundreds?"
"Did you hear 8 hundreds?"

Write on the board:

```
78x100  = 70x100 + 8x100
46x100  = _____ + _____
29x100  = _____ + _____
29x100  = _____ + _____
13x100  = _____ + _____
85x100  = _____ + _____
91x100  = _____ + _____
18x100  = _____ + _____
52x100  = _____ + _____
14x100  = _____ + _____
```

Have individual learners go to the board, say the proper statement, and fill in the spaces appropriately.

Write on the board:

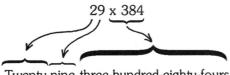

Twenty-nine three-hundred-eighty-fours

Have learners say the following, while listening very carefully to their own voices: "Twenty-nine three-hundred-eighty-fours equal 20 three-hundred-eighty-fours plus 9 three-hundred-eighty-fours."

Ask,

"Did you hear 20 three-hundred-eighty-fours?"
"Did you hear 9 three-hundred-eighty-fours?"

Write on the board:

```
29x384 =20x384 + 9x384
78x384 = _____ + _____
46x384 = _____ + _____
13x384 = _____ + _____
85x384 = _____ + _____
91x384 = _____ + _____
18x384 = _____ + _____
52x384 = _____ + _____
14x384 = _____ + _____
```

Have individual learners go to the board, say the proper statement, and fill in the spaces appropriately.

Write on the board:

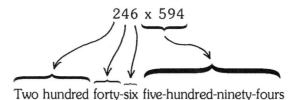

Two hundred forty-six five-hundred-ninety-fours

Have learners say the following, while listening very carefully to their own voices: "Two hundred forty-six five-hundred-ninety-fours."

Ask,
    "Did you hear 200 five-hundred-ninety-fours?"
    "Did you hear 40 five-hundred-ninety-fours?"
    "Did you hear 6 five-hundred-ninety-fours?"

Write on the board:

```
246x594=200x594 + 40x594 + 6x594
372x594=  _____ + _____ + _____
711x594=  _____ + _____ + _____
195x594=  _____ + _____ + _____
417x495=  _____ + _____ + _____
853x495=  _____ + _____ + _____
555x954=  _____ + _____ + _____
616x945=  _____ + _____ + _____
```

Have individual learners go to the board, say the proper statement, and fill in the spaces appropriately.

Write on the board:

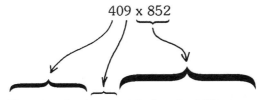

409 x 852

Four hundred nine eight-hundred-fifty-twos

Have learners say the following, while listening very carefully to their own voices: "Four hundred nine eight-hundred-fifty-twos."

Ask,

"Did you hear 400 eight-hundred-fifty-twos?"
"Did you hear 9 eight-hundred-fifty-twos?"

Write on the board:

```
409x852  = 400x852 +  9x852
605x852  = _____  + _____
702x316  = _____  + _____
504x287  = _____  + _____
208x515  = _____  + _____
707x66   = _____  + _____
905x66   = _____  + _____
103x17   = _____  + _____
```

Have individual learners go to the board, say the proper statement, and fill in the spaces appropriately.

Write on the board:

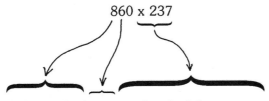

860 x 237

Eight hundred sixty two-hundred-thirty-sevens

By the same process as above, elicit the following:

860x237=800x237 + 60x237

Write on the board:

$$530 \times 672 = \rule{2em}{0.4pt} + \rule{2em}{0.4pt}$$
$$870 \times 511 = \rule{2em}{0.4pt} + \rule{2em}{0.4pt}$$
$$710 \times 304 = \rule{2em}{0.4pt} + \rule{2em}{0.4pt}$$
$$250 \times 853 = \rule{2em}{0.4pt} + \rule{2em}{0.4pt}$$
$$980 \times 45 = \rule{2em}{0.4pt} + \rule{2em}{0.4pt}$$
$$310 \times 19 = \rule{2em}{0.4pt} + \rule{2em}{0.4pt}$$
$$160 \times 86 = \rule{2em}{0.4pt} + \rule{2em}{0.4pt}$$
$$990 \times 11 = \rule{2em}{0.4pt} + \rule{2em}{0.4pt}$$

Have individual learners go to the board, say the proper statement, and fill in the spaces appropriately.

Write on the board:

$$518 \times 264 = \rule{2em}{0.4pt} + \rule{2em}{0.4pt} + \rule{2em}{0.4pt}$$
$$402 \times 100 = \rule{2em}{0.4pt} + \rule{2em}{0.4pt}$$
$$623 \times 10 = \rule{2em}{0.4pt} + \rule{2em}{0.4pt} + \rule{2em}{0.4pt}$$
$$73 \times 1,000 = \rule{2em}{0.4pt} + \rule{2em}{0.4pt}$$
$$840 \times 31 = \rule{2em}{0.4pt} + \rule{2em}{0.4pt}$$
$$31 \times 846 = \rule{2em}{0.4pt} + \rule{2em}{0.4pt}$$
$$15 \times 273 = \rule{2em}{0.4pt} + \rule{2em}{0.4pt}$$
$$203 \times 45 = \rule{2em}{0.4pt} + \rule{2em}{0.4pt}$$
$$49 \times 5 = \rule{2em}{0.4pt} + \rule{2em}{0.4pt}$$
$$704 \times 26 = \rule{2em}{0.4pt} + \rule{2em}{0.4pt}$$
$$26 \times 54 = \rule{2em}{0.4pt} + \rule{2em}{0.4pt}$$
$$370 \times 595 = \rule{2em}{0.4pt} + \rule{2em}{0.4pt}$$
$$698 \times 1,000 = \rule{2em}{0.4pt} + \rule{2em}{0.4pt} + \rule{2em}{0.4pt}$$
$$120 \times 100 = \rule{2em}{0.4pt} + \rule{2em}{0.4pt}$$
$$507 \times 465 = \rule{2em}{0.4pt} + \rule{2em}{0.4pt}$$

Have individual learners go to the board, say the proper statement, and fill in the spaces appropriately.

Have learners practice the examples in Facility Exercises #29 (Workbook II) to the level of facility; **then move on.**

Tell learners, "We already know that 57 tens equal 50 tens plus 7 tens."

Write on the board:

$$57 \times 10 = 50 \times 10 + 7 \times 10$$

Ask,
   "Fifty times ten equals ____?"
   "Seven times ten equals ____?"

Elicit the following from the learners (write it on the board):

$$57 \times 10 = \underbrace{50 \times 10} + \underbrace{7 \times 10}$$

$$= \underbrace{500 + 70}$$

$$= \quad 570$$

Tell learners, "So, 57x10 equals 570."

Ask the following questions:
"What is 67x10? 27x10? 37x10? 87x10? 23x10? 53x10? 81x10? 75x10? 49x10? 18x10? 7x10? 11x10? 30x10? 66x10? 25x10?"

Tell learners, "We already know that 57 hundreds equal 50 hundreds plus 7 hundreds."

Write on the board:

57x100=50x100 + 7x100

Ask,
"Fifty times one hundred equals _____ ?"
"Seven times one hundred equals _____ ?"

Elicit the following from the learners (write it on the board):

$$57 \times 100 = \underbrace{50 \times 100} + \underbrace{7 \times 100}$$

$$= \underbrace{5,000 + 700}$$

$$= \quad 5,700$$

Tell learners, "So, 57x100 equals 5,700."

Ask the following questions:
"What is 27x100? 47x100? 83x100? 59x100? 63x100? 92x100? 11x100? 13x100? 70x100? 10x100? 22x100? 9x100? 90x100? 43x100?"

Tell learners, "We already know that 57 thousands equal 50 thousands plus 7 thousands."

Write on the board:

57x1,000 = 50x1,000 + 7x1,000

Ask,

"Fifty times one thousand equals _____?"
"Seven times one thousand equals _____?"

Elicit the following from the learners (write it on the board):

$$57 \times 1,000 = 50 \times 1,000 + 7 \times 1,000$$

$$= 50,000 + 7,000$$

$$= 57,000$$

Tell learners, "So, 57x1,000 equals 57,000."

Ask the following questions:

"What is 97x1,000? 17x1,000? 73x1,000? 82x1,000? 12x1,000? 41x1,000? 10x1,000? 3x1,000? 60x1,000? 66x1,000? 8x1,000?"

Tell learners, "We already know that 384 hundreds equal 300 hundreds plus 80 hundreds plus 4 hundreds."

Write on the board:

384x100=300x100 + 80x100 + 4x100

Ask,

"Three hundred times one hundred equals _____ ?"
"Eighty times one hundred equals _____ ?"
"Four times one hundred equals _____ ?"

Elicit the following from the learners (write it on the board):

$$384 \times 100 = 300 \times 100 + 80 \times 100 + 4 \times 100$$

$$= 30,000 + 8,000 + 400$$

$$= 38,400$$

Tell learners, "Let's look at our results."

Write the results on the board:

$$57 \times 10 = 570$$
$$57 \times 100 = 5,700$$
$$57 \times 1,000 = 57,000$$
$$384 \times 100 = 38,400$$

Ask, "Do you see an easy way of getting the answer very quickly?"

Elicit from learners that an easy way to multiply 57 by 1,000, for example, is to count the number of zeros in 1,000, and place these three zeros on the right of 57.

Ask, "Look at our results again. Does this method of 'counting the zeros' apply to the other examples?"

Learners must do each example in the next set of exercises by the method of counting zeros.

Have learners practice the examples of Facility Exercises #30 (Workbook II) to the level of facility; **then move on.**

Illustrate the following on the board and explain all the various transformations which take us from 50x300 to 15,000.

$$50 \times 300$$
$$= 5 \times 10 \times 3 \times 100$$
$$= 5 \times 3 \times 10 \times 100$$
$$= 15 \times 1,000$$
$$= 15,000$$

Illustrate the following on the board and explain all the various transformations which take us from 7x40,000 to 280,000.

$$7 \times 40,000$$

$$= 7 \times 4 \times 10,000$$

$$= 28 \times 10,000$$

$$= 280,000$$

Illustrate the following on the board and explain all the transformations which take us from 600x7,000 to 4,200,000.

$$600 \times 7,000$$

$$= 6 \times 100 \times 7 \times 1,000$$

$$= 6 \times 7 \times 100 \times 1,000$$

$$= 42 \times 100,000$$

$$= 4,200,000$$

Write the results on the board:

$$50 \times 300 = 15,000$$
$$7 \times 40,000 = 280,000$$
$$600 \times 7,000 = 4,200,000$$

Tell learners, "Let's look at our results."

Ask, "Do you see an easy way to get the answers?"

Elicit from the learners that an easy way to multiply 600 by 7,000 (or 7,000 by 600), for example, is to first multiply the 6 by the 7, and then place the total number of zeros (in 600 and 7,000) on the right of 42.

Ask, "Does this easy method apply to the other two examples?"

Learners must do each example in Facility Exercises #31 (Workbook II) by the easy method.

Have learners practice the examples in Facility Exercises #31 to the level of facility; **then move on.**

Write on the board:

$$40 \times 100{,}000 = \text{Forty hundred-thousands}$$

$$= 4 \times 10 \times 100{,}000$$

$$= 4 \times 1{,}000{,}000 = \text{Four millions}$$

Explain to learners the transformation from forty hundred-thousands to four millions.

Write on the board:

$$60 \times 10{,}000{,}000 = \text{Sixty ten-millions}$$

$$= 6 \times 10 \times 10{,}000{,}000$$

$$= 6 \times 100{,}000{,}000 = \text{Six hundred-millions}$$

Explain to learners the transformation from sixty ten-millions to six hundred-millions.

Write on the board:

$$90 \times 1{,}000 = \text{Ninety thousands}$$

$$= 9 \times 10 \times 1{,}000$$

$$= 9 \times 10{,}000 = \text{Nine ten-thousands}$$

Summarize on the board as follows:

Forty hundred-thousands	=	Four millions
Sixty ten-millions	=	Six hundred-millions
Ninety thousands	=	Nine ten-thousands

Tell the learners to study the results above and try to complete the following statements:

Fifty ten-thousands	=	Five _____
Eighty tens	=	Eight _____
Eighty ones	=	Eight _____
Twenty millions	=	_____
Sixty hundred-millions	=	_____
Thirty-billions	=	_____
Ninety hundreds	=	_____

Have the learners practice the examples of Facility Exercises #32 (Workbook II) to the level of facility; **then move on.**

TELLING THE TRUTH WHEN
MULTIPLYING WHOLE NUMBERS

Objective: The learner will articulate each step in a multiplication example, while telling the truth regarding place value.

Write on the board:

137,698,245
_____ x7

Based on the work of the previous section, lead learners through the following expansion of 137,698,245x7:
100,000,000x7+30,000,000x7+7,000,000x7+600,000x7+90,000x7+8,000x7+200x7+40x7+5x7
=7x5+7x40+7x200+7x8,000+7x90,000+7x600,000+7x7,000,000+7x30,000,000+7x100,000,000

Take your pointer and touch the 7, the multiplication sign, and the 5 while saying, "Seven times five ones."
Learners respond, "Thirty-five ones."

Elicit from them that thirty-five ones equal thirty ones plus five ones.

Tell them, "Write the digit five in the ones' place."

Now write the following on the board:

Thirty ones = Three _____

Ask, "Thirty ones equal three what?"
Learners respond, "Tens."

Elicit from learners that they should write a small 3, representing three tens, above the digit 4 in the tens' column.

Take your pointer and touch the 7, the multiplication sign, and the 4 while saying, "Seven times four tens."
Learners respond, "Twenty-eight tens."

Ask, "Twenty-eight tens plus the three tens equal _____?"
Learners respond, "Thirty-one tens."

Elicit from them that thirty-one tens equal thirty tens plus one ten.

Tell them, "Write the digit one in the tens' place."

Now write the following on the board:

Thirty tens = Three _____

Ask, "Thirty tens equal three what?"
Learners respond, "Hundreds."

Elicit from learners that they should write a small 3, representing three hundred, above the digit 2 in the hundreds' column.

Take your pointer and touch the 7, the multiplication sign, and the 2 while saying, "Seven times two hundreds."
Learners respond, "Fourteen hundreds."

Ask, "Fourteen hundreds plus the three hundreds equal _____?"
Learners respond, "Seventeen hundreds."

Elicit from them that seventeen hundreds equal ten hundreds plus seven hundreds.

Tell them, "Write the digit seven in the hundreds' place."

Now write the following on the board:

Ten hundreds = One _____

Ask, "Ten hundreds equal one what?"
Learners respond, "Thousand."

Elicit from learners that they should write a small 1, representing one thousand, above the digit 8 in the thousands' column.

Take your pointer and touch the 7, the multiplication sign, and the 8 while saying, "Seven times eight thousands."
Learners respond, "Fifty-six thousands."

Ask, "Fifty-six thousands plus the one thousand equal _____?"
Learners respond, "Fifty-seven thousands."

Elicit from them that fifty-seven thousands equal fifty thousands plus seven thousands.

Tell them, "Write the digit seven in the thousands' place."

Now write the following on the board:

Fifty thousands = Five _____

Ask, "Fifty thousands equal five what?"
Learners respond, "Ten-thousands."

Elicit from learners that they should write a small 5, representing five ten-thousands, above the digit 9 in the ten-thousands' column.

Take your pointer and touch the 7, the multiplication sign, and the 9 while saying, "Seven times nine ten-thousands."
Learners respond, "Sixty-three ten-thousands."

Ask, "Sixty-three ten-thousands plus five ten-thousands equal _____?"
Learners respond, "Sixty-eight ten-thousands."

Elicit from them that sixty-eight ten-thousands equal sixty ten-thousands plus eight ten-thousands.

Tell them, "Write the digit eight in the ten-thousands' place."

Now write the following on the board:

Sixty ten-thousands = Six _____

Ask, "Sixty ten-thousands equal six what?"
Learners respond, "Hundred-thousands."

Elicit from learners that they should write a small 6, representing six hundred-thousands, above the digit 6 in the hundred-thousands' column.

Take your pointer and touch the 7, the multiplication sign, and the 6 while saying, "Seven times six hundred-thousands."
Learners respond, "Forty-two hundred-thousands."

Ask, "Forty-two hundred-thousands plus six hundred-thousands equal _____?"
Learners respond, "Forty-eight hundred-thousands."

Elicit from them that forty-eight hundred-thousands equal forty hundred-thousands plus eight hundred-thousands.

Tell them, "Write the digit eight in the hundred-thousands' place."

Now write the following on the board:

Forty hundred-thousands = Four _____

Ask, "Forty hundred-thousands equal four what?"
Learners respond, "Millions."

Elicit from learners that they should write a small 4, representing four millions, above the digit 7 in the millions' column.

Take your pointer and touch the 7, the multiplication sign, and the 7 while saying,

"Seven times seven millions."
Learners respond, "Forty-nine millions."

Ask, "Forty-nine millions plus four millions equal _____?"
Learners respond, "Fifty-three millions."

Elicit from them that fifty-three millions equal fifty millions plus three millions.

Tell them, "Write the digit three in the millions' place."

Now write the following on the board:

Fifty millions = Five _____

Ask, "Fifty millions equal five what?"
Learners respond, "Ten-millions."

Elicit from learners that they should write a 5, representing five ten-millions, above the digit 3 in the ten-millions' column.

Take your pointer and touch the 7, the multiplication sign, and the 3 while saying, "Seven times three ten-millions."
Learners respond, "Twenty-one ten millions."

Ask, "Twenty-one ten-millions plus five ten-millions equal _____?"
Learners respond, "Twenty-six ten-millions."

Elicit from them that twenty-six ten-millions equal twenty ten-millions plus six ten-millions.

Tell them, "Write the digit six in the ten-millions' place."

Now write the following on the board:

Twenty ten-millions = Two _____

Ask, "Twenty ten-millions equal two what?"
Learners respond, "Hundred-millions."

Elicit from learners that they should write a small 2, representing two hundred-millions, above the digit 1 in the hundred-millions' column.

Take your pointer and touch the 7, the multiplication sign, and the l while saying, "Seven times one hundred-million."
Learners respond, "Seven hundred-millions."

Ask, "Seven hundred-millions plus two hundred-millions equal _____?"
Learners respond, "Nine hundred-millions."

Tell them, "Write the digit nine in the hundred-millions' place."

The completed multiplication appears below:

```
  2 5 4 6 5 1  3 3
  1 3 7, 6 9 8, 2 4 5
                 x 7
  9 6 3, 8 8 7, 7 1 5
```

Have learners practice **telling the truth** when multiplying.

You should frequently have individuals go to the board and tell the truth when doing similar examples.

Have learners practice the examples of Facility Exercises #33 (Workbook II) to the level of facility; **then move on.**

Have each child tie a string tightly around thirty sticks and do the same with four sticks. Each child has made a total of thirty-four sticks.

Have six learners arrange their thirty-fours in six rows on a table (thirties under thirties and fours under fours).

Ask,
"How many thirty-fours do you see?" (Six thirty-fours)
"Now how many thirties do you see?" (Six thirties)
"How many fours do you see?" (Six fours)

Have the learners say three times in unison, "Six thirty-fours equal six thirties plus six fours."

Be sure learners understand from this illustration that

$$6 \times 34 = 6 \times 30 + 6 \times 4$$

six thirty-fours = six thirties plus six fours

Have them say in unison, "Six thirty-fours."

Ask them, "Six what?" (They respond, "Thirty-fours")

Tell them to repeat "Six thirty-fours" and listen carefully to their own voices.

Ask, "If you say, 'six thirty-fours' can you 'hear' 'six thirties' and 'six fours'?"

Write on the board:

$$37 \times 258 = 30 \times 258 + 7 \times 258$$

Tell learners they already know how to expand 37x258 as shown on the board.

Write on the board:

7x258

Tell learners that 7x258 is part of the expansion of 37x258.

Have them say in unison, "Seven two-hundred-fifty-eights."

Ask them, "Seven what?" (They respond, "Two-hundred-fifty-eights")

Tell them to repeat "seven two-hundred-fifty-eights" and listen carefully to their own voices.

Now ask, "If you say, 'seven two-hundred-fifty-eights,' can you hear 'seven two-hundreds,' 'seven fifties,' and 'seven eights'?"

Write on the board:

7x258 = 7x200 + 7x50 + 7x8

Write on the board:

30x258

Have learners say in unison, "Thirty two-hundred-fifty-eights."

Ask them, "Thirty what?" (They respond, "Two-hundred-fifty-eights")

Tell them to repeat "thirty two-hundred-fifty-eights" and listen carefully to their own voices.

Now ask, "If you say, 'thirty two-hundred-fifty-eights,' can you hear 'thirty two-hundreds,' 'thirty fifties,' and 'thirty eights'?"

Write on the board:

7x258 = 7x200 + 7x50 + 7x8
30x258 = 30x200 + 30x50 + 30x8

37x258 = 30x258 + 7x258 = 7x8 + 7x50 + 7x200 + 30x8 + 30x50 + 30x200

Elicit from learners the following:

7x8 = 56	30x8 = 240
7x50 = 350	30x50 = 1,500
7x200 = 1,400	30x200 = 6,000

Write on the board:

258
x37

Direct learners as follows:

1. Look for 7x8 in the example on the board. Since the answer is fifty-six, write 56 under the 37.

2. Look for 7x50 in the example on the board. Since the answer is three hundred fifty, write 350 appropriately (line up according to place value) under the 56.

3. Look for 7x200 in the example on the board. Since the answer is one thousand four hundred, write 1,400 appropriately (line up according to place value) under the 350.

The board work now looks like this:

```
  258
  x37
   56
  350
1,400
```

Continue to direct learners as follows:

1. Look for 30x8 on the board. Since the answer is two hundred forty, write 240 appropriately under the 1,400.

2. Look for 30x50 on the board. Since the answer is one thousand five hundred, write 1,500 appropriately under 240.

3. Look for 30x200 on the board. Since the answer is six thousand, write 6,000 appropriately under 1,500.

The board work eventually looks like this:

```
  258
  x37
   56
  350
1,400
  240
1,500
6,000
9,546
```

Show the following on the board:

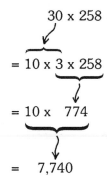

$$30 \times 258$$

$$= 10 \times 3 \times 258$$

$$= 10 \times \quad 774$$

$$= \quad 7,740$$

Use the above board-work to explain that to do the multiplication, 30x258, we can multiply 258 by 3 (without telling the truth) first; then multiply the answer by 10. The multiplication of 258 by 7 can also be done without telling the truth.

Show the following on the board:

Multiplication of 258 by 7

```
      4 5
     258
     _x7_
   1,806
```

"Long way multiplication"
```
        258
      x 37
          56
7x258 { 350 } =1,806
       1,400
         240
30x258 {1,500} =7,740
        6,000
       9,546
```

Multiplication of 258 by 30

```
      1 2
     258
     _x30_
   7,740
```

Write the zero first (this shows multiplication by 10) then multiply by 3.

"Short-cut multiplication"
```
          12
          45
         258
         _x37_
7x258  → 1,806
30x258 → 7,740
37x258 → 9,546
```

Use the above board work to "make sense" of short-cut multiplication.

Write on the board:

439	862	705	6,007	3,819
x76	x43	x69	x25	x48

Have learners do these multiplications the long way.

Have learners practice the same multiplications (above) by means of the short-cut method without telling the truth (they must make no reference to place value). Learners are to do each example in Facility Exercises #34 (Workbook II) by the short-cut method without telling the truth.

Have them practice the examples of Facility Exercises #34 to the level of facility; **then move on.**

Facility Exercises #35 are the third of nine Mixed Practice experiences for the learners in Workbook II.

Write on the board:

    258
    x37

Let's tell the truth the short-cut way.

First we multiply by the seven.

Seven times eight equals fifty-six.

Write the digit 6 in the ones' place, and write the digit 5 (representing fifty) above the 5 in the tens' place.

Seven times fifty equals three hundred fifty, plus the fifty equals four hundred.

Write the digit zero in the tens' place, and write the digit 4 (representing four hundred) above the 2 in the hundreds' column.

Seven times two hundred equals one thousand four hundred, plus the four hundred equals one thousand eight hundred.

Write the digit 8 (representing eight hundred) in the hundreds' place, and write the digit 1 in the thousands' place.

The work now looks like this:

                45
              258
             _x37_
            1,806

Next, we multiply by the thirty.

Thirty times eight equals two hundred forty.

Write the digit zero in the ones' place; the digit 4 (representing forty) in the tens' place; and the digit 2 (representing two hundred) in the hundreds' column above the 2 (and above the 4).

Thirty times fifty equals one thousand five hundred, plus the two hundred equals one thousand seven hundred.

Write the digit 7 (representing seven hundred) in the hundreds' place, and write the digit 1 (representing one thousand) above the thousands' column.

Thirty times two hundred equals six thousands, plus the one thousand equals seven thousands.

Write the digit 7 (representing seven thousands) in the thousands' place.

Write on the board:

```
      1 2
       45
      258
     _x37
    1,806
    7,740
```

Next, we add up the two numbers: 1,806 and 7,740.

The work finally looks like this:

```
      1 2
       45
      258
     _x37
    1,806
    7,740
    9,546
```

The answer is 9,546.

Write on the board:

436	768	597	675
x72	x43	x86	x69

Have learners practice the multiplication examples above, by telling the truth the short-cut way.

We will now have learners do multiplication examples the short-cut way, without referring to place value (i.e. without telling the truth) as was done earlier.

Write the following on the board:

648x529 = 600x529 + 40x529 + 8x529

Tell learners we already know how to expand 648x529 as shown on the board. Have them multiply 8x529 and 40x529. Their work should appear as below.

```
  2 7              1 3
  529              529
   x8              x40
4,232           21,160
```
— **write one zero first**

Remind learners to multiply 600x529 **by writing two zeros first**, then multiplying by 6. Their work should appear as below.

```
   1 5
    529
   x600
 317,400
```
— **write two zeros first**

Write on the board as follows:

648x529 = 600x529 + 40x529 + 8x529

= 317,400 + 21,160 + 4,232

= 342,792

Demonstrate the following short-cut for the above procedures on the board:

```
    1 5
    1 3
    2 7
    529
   x648
  4,232  ←——————— 8x529
 21,160  ←——————— 40x529
317,400  ←——————— 600x529
342,792  ←——————— 648x529
```

Lead learners through the multiplications below:

```
  6 4             5 2
  7 5             5 2
   286             684
  x890            x706
 25,740          4,104
228,800        478,800
254,540        482,904
```

Be sure learners see that when multiplying the 684 by the 700 in 706, they must first write two zeros then multiply by 7.

Write on the board:

247	378	835	847
x96	x643	x304	x760

Have learners practice these multiplications by means of the short-cut and without regard to place value (without telling the truth).

Learners are to do the examples in Facility Exercises #36 (Workbook II), by the multiplication algorithm shown above.

Have learners practice the examples of Facility Exercises #36 to the level of facility; **then move on.**

USING MULTIPLICATION TO SOLVE WORD PROBLEMS

Objective: Children will solve word problems using multiplication.

We now apply multiplication to word problems, since this experience will prepare learners for our original contextual approach to long division.

The use of fingers, for teaching the application of multiplication to the word problems below, will be very effective due to the learners' experience with our finger activity for rapidly teaching the multiplication facts.

Lead your learners through the problems below.

If you pretend each one of your fingers is a bundle of six sticks, then four fingers equal how many sticks?

If you pretend each one of your fingers is six chairs, then four fingers equal how many chairs?

If you pretend each one of your fingers is $6, then four fingers equal how much money?

If you pretend each one of your fingers is a box with eight books, then nine fingers equal how many books?

If you pretend each one of your fingers is a game which costs $7, then five fingers would equal how many games? How much would the five games cost?

If one game costs $6, then how much do five games cost?

If you pretend each one of your fingers is a pen which costs $4, then seven fingers would equal how many pens? How much would the seven pens cost?

If one pen costs $5, then how much do ten pens cost? Fifteen pens? Twenty-three pens? Thirty-one pens?

If you pretend each one of your fingers is a radio which costs $87, then eight fingers would equal how many radios? How much would the eight radios cost?

If one radio costs $145, how much do three radios cost? Seventeen radios? Sixty-four radios?

If you pretend each finger is $486, then nine fingers equal how much money? Twenty-four fingers equal how much money?

If you pretend each one of your fingers is a camera which costs $479, then six fingers would equal how many cameras? How much would the six cameras cost?

If one camera costs $368, how much do eight cameras cost? Forty-seven cameras? Fifty-eight cameras?

What is the cost of 67 TV sets if each one costs $698?

What is the cost of 1,000 chairs if each one costs $43?

If one desk cost $236, what is the cost of 73 desks?

If one book costs $36, what is the cost of 100,000 books? 100 books? 10,000 books? 10 books? One book?

Now that learners understand the use of multiplication to solve word problems, it is important that you compare the method of solution in this section with that which appears on page four.

Learners will truly appreciate multiplication when they realize, for example, that the cost of 86 items at $497 each can be found by multiplication of 497 by 86, rather than by lining up 497, in writing, 86 times and adding them up.

Have learners practice the examples of Facility Exercises #37 (Workbook II) to the level of facility; **then move on.**

FOR THE APPRECIATION OF LONG DIVISION

Objective: Learners will ask you to teach them long division.

Write on the board:

$$2\overline{)25}$$

Have learners do this example by means of repeated subtraction (as they did in the section entitled "Short Division with Remainder").

They will find they can subtract twelve 2's from 25 and leave a remainder of 1.

Write on the board:

$$3\overline{)50}$$

Have learners do this example by means of repeated subtraction.

They will find they can subtract sixteen 3's from 50 and leave a remainder of 2.

Write on the board:

$$32\overline{)175}$$

Have learners do this example by means of repeated subtraction.

They will find they can subtract five 32's from 175, and leave a remainder of 15.

Write on the board:

$$23\overline{)343}$$

Have learners do this example by means of repeated subtraction.

They will find they can subtract fourteen 23's from 343 and leave a remainder of 21.

Write on the board:

$$34\overline{)94{,}671}$$

Tell learners to do this example without revealing in any way that you realize the absurdity of this request.

You must try not to laugh or even smile (it will be difficult) as you elicit responses to this example from the learners.

After they have done a few (seven or eight) steps ask,

"Do you think you will soon be finished?" (Learners will respond, "NO!")
"Will you be finished in about ten minutes?"
"Would a half-hour be enough time to finish?"
"If I let you finish this for home work, about how long would it take?"
"Would you like to take a month to finish this, or would you like a short-cut which could take you less than ten minutes?"

Tell learners that the short-cut for repeated subtractions which take a long time is called long division.

Emphasize that long division is a short-cut.

Now ask, "Do you want to learn long division?" (All learners say, "YES!")

Tell learners you will do the long division problem on the board (94,671÷34) using long division in the near future.

In fact, this same problem is used for the introduction of long-division in the section of this book entitled, "Telling the Truth About Long Division."

TELLING THE TRUTH ABOUT LONG DIVISION

Objective: The learner will do long division examples with dividends up to six digits and divisors up to three digits.

The long division techniques and dialogues in this section have been developed and sharpened over many years of classroom experience. By these methods, trained teachers have delivered competence in long division to second graders from low to high socio-economic backgrounds. They ensure that learners understand it the first time they experience it.

Be very sure that the learners are skilled in the following prerequisites for long division before proceeding further:
1. Place value;
2. Comparing numbers;
3. Subtraction skills;
4. Multiplication facts;
5. Rapid mental multiplication of a whole number by a power of ten;
6. Multiplication skills;
7. Short division using multiplication facts; and
8. Some experience with simple word problems which require multiplication.

Your major objective in your first few lessons on long division is that it **must make sense** to the learners.

One of the most significant and original notions in our approach to this objective is the use of a verbal problem for ensuring that every step in the long division process makes sense to learners, **during their very first experience** of this traditionally difficult topic.

As you elicit the various steps from the learners in the example below, be sure you do not have them merely being spectators, as they watch you do all the work.

You must do all the necessary eliciting, but they must be required to have the problem on paper before them, and to perform all the necessary multiplications and subtractions; as well as respond to your questions. In this manner, they will be

71

actively engaged in long division, even if it is the first one they ever saw.

Warn them to write **very neatly** and insist that their work on paper must look "even better than" your work on the board.

Write the following problem on the board:
Your principal has $275 and wishes to buy some workbooks for her school. How many can she buy if the cost of each book is $4?

Have the learners read the problem.

Now write the following on the board:

$$4\overline{)275}$$

Tell learners that the number under the line is called the dividend (have them say "dividend"), and the number on the left is called the divisor (have them say "divisor").

Have them name each place value in the dividend.
Learners respond, "Ones, tens, hundreds."

Tell learners that there is a question for each value in the dividend and they must know how to ask each one.

Insist that each learner pretends to be the principal, as the questions are being asked.
The questions are listed below:
1. Hundreds' place: "Can I buy one hundred books?"
2. Tens' place: "Can I buy ten books?"
3. One's place: "Can I buy one book?"

Have learners practice asking the above questions to the level of facility.

Now return to the first question: "Can I buy one hundred books?"

Elicit from the learners that the cost of one hundred books is $400. This is more than the amount of money ($275) available. Hence no learner can buy one hundred books.

The board (and learners') work now looks like this:

$$4\overset{x}{\overline{)275}} \qquad 400$$

Insist that learners write 400 to the right of the division as appears above.

The little "x" above the two in the hundreds' place means that each learner buys "zero hundreds" of books, since one hundred books cost too much. It also means each learner cannot buy any books in the hundreds' place.

Since each learner cannot buy 100 books, we move to the tens' place and ask, "Can I buy ten books?"

Elicit from learners that the cost of ten books is $40. This is less than the amount of money ($275) available. Hence each learner can buy ten books.

The board (and learners') work now looks like this:

$$4\overline{)275} \qquad\qquad \begin{array}{r} 400 \\ 40 \end{array}$$

Now consider the digits: 0, 1, 2, 3, 4, 5, 6, 7, 8, 9.
Explain to learners that in the tens' place, these digits represent 0 tens, 1 ten, 2 tens, 3 tens, and so on, up to 9 tens.

Tell them that since they can buy 10 books each, perhaps they can buy 20, or 30, or 40, and so on, up to 90 books each.
So the question is this: What are the **maximum tens** of books each learner can buy?

To estimate the maximum tens of books, we must use the digit in the divisor, 4, and the first digit, 2, in the dividend 275, and ask the question, "Four into two?"

Since four "does not go into" two, we must use the digit in the divisor, 4, and the first two digits, 27, in the dividend, and ask the question, "Four into twenty-seven?"

Tell learners that, in fact, we are really asking the question, "Four into two hundred seventy?"
The answer to "four into twenty-seven" is six (4 into 270 is approximately 60).

Have learners understand this "six" means that from among the choices of 10 through 90 books, they must see if they can buy 60 books.

Have them see, by multiplication, that the cost of 60 books is $240.
This is less than $275; so the maximum tens of books which can be bought is 6 (which means 60 books).

The board work now looks like this:

$$\begin{array}{r} \overset{\text{x6}}{} \\ 4\overline{)275} \\ -\ 240 \\ \hline 35 \end{array} \qquad\qquad \begin{array}{r} 400 \\ 40 \end{array}$$

The board work shows learners that after 60 books have been bought, $35 are left.

Ask, "Can you buy more books out of the remaining $35?"

Elicit from learners that they must now move over to the ones' place and ask, "Can I buy one book?" Since one book costs $4, they can.

Now let us return to the digits 0, 1, 2, 3, 4, 5, 6, 7, 8, 9.

Explain to learners that in the ones' place, these digits represent zero, one, two, three, and so on, up to nine.

Tell them that since they can buy one book each, perhaps they can buy 2, or 3, or 4, and so on, up to 9 books each.
So the question is this: What are the **maximum ones** of books each learner can buy?

To estimate the maximum ones of books, we must use the digit in the divisor, 4, and the first digit, 3, in 35 and ask the question, "Four into three?"

Since four does not go into three, we must use the digit, 4, and the two digits, 35, and ask the question, "Four into thirty-five?"
The answer to the question is eight.

Have learners agree that since we are in the ones' place, the "eight" means that each learner must try to buy eight books.

Have them see, by multiplication, that the cost of 8 books is $32.
This is less than $35, so the maximum ones of books which can be bought is 8 (which means 8 books).

The board work finally looks like this:

$$
\begin{array}{r}
_{\times}68 \\
4\overline{)275} \\
-\,240 \\
\hline
35 \\
-\,32 \\
\hline
3
\end{array}
\qquad
\begin{array}{r}
400 \\
40 \\
4
\end{array}
$$

Ask, "Can you buy any more books?" The board work shows that 68 books have been bought and $3 are left over.

Tell learners that the answer to this long division is called the quotient, and the amount left over is the remainder.

Have them understand that when the dividend is 275 and the divisor is 4, the quotient is 68 and the remainder is 3.

Have learners **check** their work by means of the following word problem: Your principal has bought 68 books at $4 each and has $3 left over. How much money did she have originally?
Do they end up with the original amount of money?

Virtually all learners, who have the prerequisite skills, will experience a very meaningful introduction to long division, by means of this approach.

Elicit the steps to the following long division examples, by means of the above procedures.

Make up a verbal problem for each example.

Learners must check each answer after it is completed.

$$3\overline{)208} \qquad 4\overline{)973} \qquad 7\overline{)616}$$

$$3\overline{)973} \qquad 5\overline{)324} \qquad 8\overline{)973}$$

$$4\overline{)391} \qquad 2\overline{)195} \qquad 6\overline{)123}$$

CAUTION: Do not assign long divisions for homework until learners have acquired skill through classroom involvement. This is necessary, since confusion often develops when the division techniques of a "helpful" parent or friend are different from those being used in the classroom.

As you lead learners through the various steps in the long division below, you must do all the necessary eliciting.
However, they must be required to have the problem on paper before them, and to perform all the necessary multiplications and subtractions; as well as respond to your questions.
In this manner, they will be actively engaged with the problems.

Warn them to write **very neatly**, and insist that their work on paper must look better than your work on the board.

Write the following problem on the board:
Your principal has $94,671 to buy chairs at $34 each. How many chairs can she purchase?

Have the learners read the problem.

Now write the following on the board:

$$34\overline{)94,671}$$

Have the learners name each place value in the dividend.
Learners respond, "Ten-thousands, thousands, hundreds, tens, ones."

Have each learner pretend to be the principal, as the group practices asking the questions below (in unison) to the level of facility:

1. Ten-thousands' place: "Can I buy ten-thousand chairs?"
2. Thousands' place: "Can I buy one thousand chairs?"
3. Hundreds' place: "Can I buy one hundred chairs?"
4. Tens' place: "Can I buy ten chairs?"
5. Ones' place: "Can I buy one chair?"

Have learners return to the first question and ask, "Can I buy ten-thousand chairs?"

Elicit from learners that each one of them is unable to purchase ten-thousand chairs.

The board (and learners') work now looks like this:

$$\overset{\text{x}}{34\overline{)94{,}671}} \qquad\qquad 340{,}000$$

Have learners explain the meaning of the "x" above the ten-thousands' place.

Now have them ask the question for the thousands' place: "Can I buy one thousand chairs?"

Elicit from learners that each one of them can buy one thousand chairs.

At this point, have them consider the digits 0, 1, 2, 3, 4, 5, 6, 7, 8, 9. Since we are in the thousands' place, these digits represent 0 thousands, 1 thousand, 2 thousands, 3 thousands, and so on, up to 9 thousands.

Tell learners that since they can buy 1,000 chairs each, perhaps they can buy 2,000, or 3,000, or 4,000, and so on, up to 9,000 chairs each.
So the question is this: What are the **maximum thousands** of chairs each learner can buy?

Tell learners that to estimate the maximum thousands of chairs, we must use **the first digit of the divisor**, 3, and the first digit, 9, of the dividend 94,671, and ask the question, "Three into nine?"

Tell learners that, in fact, we are really asking the question, "Thirty into ninety-thousand?"
The answer to "three into nine" is three (which means 30 into 90,000 is 3,000).

Have learners see this "three" as meaning that from among the choices of 1,000 chairs through 9,000 chairs, they must see if they can buy 3,000 chairs.

Elicit from learners that
1. the cost of 3,000 chairs is greater than the amount of money available; and
2. the maximum thousands of chairs one of them can purchase is 2 (2,000 chairs).

The board (and learners') work now looks like this:

$$
\begin{array}{r}
\overset{\text{x2}}{34\overline{)94{,}671}} \\
-\underline{68{,}000} \\
26{,}671
\end{array}
\qquad\qquad
\begin{array}{r}
340{,}000 \\
34{,}000
\end{array}
$$

Elicit from learners that after each of them has bought 2,000 chairs, they still have $26,671 each.

Ask, "Can you buy more chairs?"

Elicit from learners that they must move over to the hundreds' place and ask, "Can I buy one hundred chairs?"
Since learners can buy 100 chairs each, perhaps everyone can buy 200, or 300, or 400, and so on, up to 900 chairs.
So the question is this: What are the **maximum hundreds** of chairs each learner can buy?

Tell learners that to estimate the maximum hundreds of chairs, we must use the **first digit of the divisor**, 3, **and the first digit, 2, in 26,671**, and ask the question, "Three into two?"
Since three does not go into two, we must use the first digit of the divisor, 3, and **the first two digits, 26, in 26,671**, and ask the question, "Three into twenty-six?"

Tell learners that, in fact, we are really asking the question, "Thirty into twenty-six thousand?"
The answer to "three into twenty-six" is eight (which means 30 into 26,000 is approximately 800).

Have learners see that this "eight" means that from among the choices of 100 through 900 chairs, they must see if they can buy 800 chairs.

Elicit from learners that
1. the cost of 800 chairs is greater than the amount of money available; and
2. the maximum hundreds of chairs one of them can purchase is 7 (700 chairs).

The board (and learners') work now looks like this:

$$
\begin{array}{r}
_{x}2,7 \\
\hline
34\overline{)94,671} \\
-68,000 \\
\hline
26,671 \\
-23,800 \\
\hline
2,871
\end{array}
\qquad
\begin{array}{r}
340,000 \\
34,000 \\
3,400
\end{array}
$$

Elicit from learners that after each of them has bought 700 chairs, they still have $2,871 each.

Ask, "Can you buy any more chairs?"

Elicit from learners that they must move over to the tens' place and ask, "Can I buy ten chairs?"

Since each learner can buy ten chairs, have them return to the digits 0, 1, 2, 3, 4, 5, 6, 7, 8, 9 and conclude that perhaps they can buy 20, or 30, or 40, and so on, up to 90 chairs each.

So the question is this: What are the **maximum tens** of chairs each learner can buy?

Tell learners that to estimate the maximum tens of chairs, we must use the **first digit of the divisor**, 3, and the **first two digits, 28, in 2,871** (since the first digit of the divisor, 3, does not go into the first digit, 2, of 2,871).

Tell learners that, in fact, we are really asking the question, "Thirty into two thousand eight hundred?"
The answer to "three into twenty-eight" is nine (30 into 2,800 is approximately 90).

Elicit from learners that this "nine" means they must see if they can buy 90 chairs (from among the choices of 10 chairs through 90 chairs).

Have learners conclude, on their own, that the cost of 90 chairs is greater than the $2,871 they have left.

Elicit from them that they can each purchase 80 more chairs. The maximum tens of chairs which each learner can purchase is 8 (80 chairs).

The board (and learners') work now looks like this:

$$
\begin{array}{r}
{}_{\times}2{,}78 \\
\hline
34\overline{)94{,}671} \\
-\,68{,}000 \\
\hline
26{,}671 \\
-\,23{,}800 \\
\hline
2{,}871 \\
-\,2{,}720 \\
\hline
151
\end{array}
\qquad
\begin{array}{r}
340{,}000 \\
34{,}000 \\
3{,}400 \\
340
\end{array}
$$

Elicit from learners that after each of them has bought 80 chairs, they still have $151 each.

Ask, "Can you buy any more chairs?"

Elicit from learners that they must move over to the ones' place and ask, "Can I buy one chair?"

Have them return to the digits 0, 1, 2, 3, 4, 5, 6, 7, 8, 9 and conclude that perhaps they can buy 2, or 3, or 4, and so on, up to 9 chairs each.
So the question is this: What are the **maximum ones** of chairs each learner can buy?

Elicit from them that to estimate the maximum ones of chairs, we must again use the **first digit of the divisor**, 3, and the **first two digits, 15, in 151** (since the first digit of the divisor, 3, does not go into the first digit, 1 of 151).

Tell learners that, in fact, we are really asking the question, "Thirty into one hundred fifty?" The answer to "three into fifteen" is five (30 into 151 is approximately 5).

Elicit from learners this "five" means that from among the choices of 1 chair through 9 chairs, they must see if they can buy five chairs.

Since the cost of five chairs is greater than $151, elicit from them that they can each purchase 4 more chairs. The maximum ones of chairs which each learner can purchase is 4.

The board (and learners') work finally looks like this:

$$
\begin{array}{r}
{}_{\times}2{,}784 \\
\hline
34\overline{)94{,}671} \\
-\,68{,}000 \\
\hline
26{,}671 \\
-\,23{,}800 \\
\hline
2{,}871 \\
-\,2{,}720 \\
\hline
151 \\
-\,136 \\
\hline
15
\end{array}
\qquad
\begin{array}{r}
340{,}000 \\
34{,}000 \\
3{,}400 \\
340 \\
34
\end{array}
$$

Ask, "Can you buy any more chairs?"
The board work shows that 2,784 chairs have been bought and $15 are left over.

Have learners understand that when the dividend is 94,671 and the divisor is 34, the quotient is 2,784 and the remainder is 15.

Have learners **check** their work by means of the following word problem: Your principal has bought 2,784 chairs, at $34 each, and has $15 left over. How much money did she have originally?

Elicit the steps to the following long division examples, by means of the above procedures.

Make up a verbal problem for each example.

Learners must check each example after it is completed.

$23\overline{)17{,}171}$	$54\overline{)14{,}673}$	$63\overline{)217{,}735}$
$32\overline{)84{,}731}$	$26\overline{)9{,}415}$	$79\overline{)5{,}372}$
$47\overline{)39{,}645}$	$9\overline{)7{,}443}$	$76\overline{)999{,}999}$
$67\overline{)867}$	$23\overline{)867}$	$16\overline{)867}$
$47\overline{)98}$	$31\overline{)74}$	$23\overline{)37}$

CAUTION: Do not assign long divisions for homework until learners have acquired skill through classroom involvement. This is necessary, since confusion often develops when the division techniques of a "helpful" parent or friend are different from those being used in the classroom.

As you lead learners through the various steps in the long division below, you must do all the necessary eliciting.
However, they must be required to have the problem on paper before them, and to perform all the necessary multiplications and subtractions; as well as respond to your questions.
In this manner, they will be actively engaged with the problem.

Warn them to write **very neatly**, and insist that their work on paper must look better than your work on the board.

Write the following problem on the board:
Miss Johns has $16,032 to purchase calculators for her store. If the cost of one calculator is $8, how many can she buy?

Now write on the board:

$$8\overline{)16,032}$$

Elicit the following:
1. They cannot buy 10,000 calculators.
2. They can buy 1,000 calculators.
3. The maximum thousands of calculators they can buy is 2 (2,000 calculators).
4. After they have bought 2,000 calculators, they have $32 left over.
5. They cannot buy 100 calculators.
6. The maximum hundreds of calculators they can buy is 0 (0 hundreds).
7. They cannot buy 10 calculators.
8. The maximum tens of calculators they can buy is 0 (0 tens).

The board work now looks like this:

$$
\begin{array}{r}
{\scriptstyle \times}2{,}00 \\
8\overline{)16{,}032} \\
-\,16{,}000 \\
\hline
32
\end{array}
\qquad
\begin{array}{r}
80{,}000 \\
8{,}000 \\
800 \\
80
\end{array}
$$

Elicit the following from the learners:
1. They can buy one calculator.
2. The maximum ones of calculators they can buy is 4.
3. After they have bought 4 calculators, they have no money left over.

The board work finally looks like this:

$$\begin{array}{r} {}_{\times}2{,}004 \\ \hline 8\overline{)16{,}032} \\ -\,16{,}000 \\ \hline 32 \\ -\,32 \\ \hline 0 \end{array} \qquad \begin{array}{r} 80{,}000 \\ 8{,}000 \\ 800 \\ 80 \\ 8 \end{array}$$

The board work shows that 2,004 calculators have been bought.

Have learners **check** their work by means of the following word problem: Miss Johns has bought 2,004 calculators at \$8 each and has no money left. How much money did she have?

Elicit the steps to the following long division examples (make up a verbal problem for each one):

$3\overline{)1{,}518}$	$6\overline{)1{,}828}$	$7\overline{)21{,}017}$
$23\overline{)9{,}263}$	$43\overline{)3{,}023}$	$27\overline{)54{,}081}$
$48\overline{)24{,}207}$	$7\overline{)5{,}605}$	$9\overline{)2{,}705}$
$81\overline{)867}$	$4\overline{)93}$	$3\overline{)92}$
$68\overline{)48{,}008}$	$9\overline{)19}$	$63\overline{)3{,}975}$

CAUTION: Do not assign long divisions for homework until learners have acquired skill through classroom involvement. This is necessary, since confusion often develops when the division techniques of a "helpful" parent or friend are different from those being used in the classroom.

As you lead learners through the various steps in the long division examples of Facility Exercises #38 you must do all the necessary eliciting.
However, they must be required to have the problem on paper before them, and to perform all the necessary multiplications and subtractions; as well as respond to your questions.
In this manner, they will be actively engaged with the problem.

Warn them to write **very neatly**, and insist that their work on paper must look better than your work on the board.

Have learners practice the examples of Facility Exercises #38 (Workbook II) to the level of facility; **then move on.**

Facility Exercises #39 are the fourth of nine Mixed Practice experiences for the learners in Workbook II.

Write the following problem on the board:
A car manufacturer wishes to spend $271,965 to buy car radios at $68 each. How many car radios can they buy?

Now write on the board:

$$68\overline{)271{,}965}$$

Elicit the following from the learners:
1. They cannot buy 100,000 radios.
2. They cannot buy 10,000 radios.
3. They can buy 1,000 radios.
4. The maximum thousands of radios they can buy is 3 (3,000 radios).
5. After they have bought 3,000 radios, they have $67,965 left.
6. They can buy 100 radios out of the remaining $67,965.

The work now looks like this:

```
        xx3
  68)271,965           6,800,000
    -204,000             680,000
      67,965              68,000
                           6,800
```

Elicit from learners that since they can buy 100 radios with $67,965, they must now find the maximum hundreds of radios that can be bought.

Have learners notice that, at this point, something unexpected happens.
To estimate the maximum hundreds of radios which can be bought, we use the first digit in the divisor, 6, and the first digit, 6, in 67,965.
Six goes into six once.
The answer to this question is "one."
What does "one" mean?
Should we try to buy one hundred radios since we are in the hundreds' place?

Elicit from learners that the cost of 100 radios ($6,800) is so much less than the $67,965, that they could buy many more hundreds of radios.

Lead them to conclude that
1. the $67,965 is closer to the cost of 1,000 radios, than to the cost of 100 radios;
2. they cannot buy 1,000 radios (so they must buy less than 1,000);
3. of the possibilities, 100 through 900 radios, the one which is closest to 1,000 is 900;

4. they must try to buy 900 radios; and
5. the maximum hundreds of radios which can be bought is 9 (900 radios).

Another way of resolving the question of whether the "one" means one hundred, or one thousand, is to look at the question, "Six into six?" as meaning sixty into sixty thousand.
This equals one thousand.
But we cannot buy 1,000 radios; so we try to buy 900.

Elicit from learners that they can buy 10 radios out of the remaining $6,765.

The work now looks like this:

$$
\begin{array}{r}
\text{xx }3,9 \\
68\overline{)271,965} \\
-\,204,000 \\
\hline
67,965 \\
-\,61,200 \\
\hline
6,765
\end{array}
\qquad
\begin{array}{r}
6,800,000 \\
680,000 \\
68,000 \\
6,800 \\
680
\end{array}
$$

Elicit from learners that in estimating the maximum tens of radios which can be bought, the first digit of the divisor, 6, goes into the first digit, 6, of 6,765, once. What does this "one" mean? Ten radios or one hundred radios?

Elicit from learners that the cost of ten radios ($680) is so much less than the $6,765, that they could buy many more tens of radios.

Lead them to conclude that
1. the $6,765 is closer to the cost of 100 radios, than to the cost of 10 radios;
2. they cannot buy 100 radios (so they must buy less than 100);
3. of the possibilities, 10 through 90 radios, the one which is closest to 100 is 90;
4. they must try to buy 90 radios; and
5. the maximum tens of radios which can be bought is 9 (90 radios).

Another way of determining whether the "one" means ten, or one hundred, is to look at the question, "Six into six?" as meaning sixty into six thousand.
This equals one hundred.
But we cannot buy 100 radios; so we try to buy 90.

Elicit from learners that they can buy one radio out of the remaining $645.

The work now looks like this:

```
            x x 3 , 9 9
        68 ) 274,965              6,800,000
          − 204,000                 680,000
            67,965                   68,000
          − 61,200                    6,800
             6,765                      680
           − 6,120                       68
              645
```

Elicit from learners that in estimating the maximum ones of radios which can be bought, the first digit of the divisor, 6, goes into the first digit, 6, of 645, once. What does this "one" mean? One radio or ten radios?

Elicit from learners that the cost of one radio ($68) is so much less than $645, that they could buy many more ones of radios.

Lead them to conclude that
1. the $645 is closer to the cost of 10 radios than to the cost of 1 radio;
2. they cannot buy 10 radios (so they must buy less than 10);
3. of the possibilities, 1 through 9 radios, the one which is closest to 10 is 9;
4. they must try to buy 9 radios; and
5. the maximum ones of radios which can be bought is 9 (9 radios).

Another way of determining whether the "one" means one or ten is to look at the question, "Six into six?" as meaning sixty into six hundred.
This equals ten.
But we cannot buy 10 radios, so we try to buy 9.

The work finally looks like this:

```
            x x 3 , 9 9 9
        68 ) 274,965
          − 204,000
            67,965
          − 61,200
             6,765
           − 6,120
              645
            − 612
               33
```

Have learners conclude that 3,999 radios have been bought and $33 are left over.

Have learners **check** their work by means of the following word problem: A car manufacturer bought 3,999 radios at $68 each and has $33 left over. How much money did he have originally?

Elicit the steps to the following long division examples (make up a verbal problem for each one):

$$45\overline{)35,567} \qquad 54\overline{)22,679} \qquad 84\overline{)24,422}$$

$$40\overline{)24,373} \qquad 38\overline{)34,562} \qquad 76\overline{)531,605}$$

$$83\overline{)82,917} \qquad 63\overline{)5,638} \qquad 86\overline{)696,342}$$

$$38\overline{)22,789} \qquad 62\overline{)57,660} \qquad 18\overline{)70,287}$$

Have learners practice the examples of Facility Exercises #40 (Workbook II) to the level of facility; **then move on.**

Tell learners that, eventually, they should be able to do long division examples without associating them with verbal problems.
An example is described below.

Write the following problem on the board:

$$286\overline{)105,200}$$

Explain to learners that the above long division example will be done without turning it into a verbal problem.

Tell them that there will be different types of questions for each place value in the dividend, and they must know how to ask each one.

The first question is, "Can I take one hundred-thousand 286's out of 105,200?" (No)
The second question is, "Can I take ten thousand 286's out of 105,200?" (No)
The third question is, "Can I take one thousand 286's out of 105,200?" (No)
The fourth question is, "Can I take one hundred 286's out of 105,200?" (Yes)

Now since we can take one hundred 286's out; then perhaps we can take out two hundred 286's; or three hundred 286's; or four hundred 286's; and so on, up to nine hundred 286's.

In order to estimate the **maximum hundreds** of 286 we can take out, we use the first digit, 2, in the divisor and the first two digits, 10, in the dividend.

Since 2 goes into 10 five times, we will see if we can take out five hundred 286's (we cannot).

Since five hundred 286's is too large, we will try to take out four hundred 286's (we cannot).

Since four hundred 286's is too large, we will try to take out three hundred 286's (we can).

So the maximum hundreds of 286 we can take out is 3 (three hundred).

After taking out the maximum hundreds of 286, we have 19,400 left over.

The work now looks like this:

$$
\begin{array}{r}
3 \\
286\overline{)105{,}200} \\
-\ 85{,}800 \\
\hline
19{,}400
\end{array}
\qquad
\begin{array}{r}
28{,}600{,}000 \\
2{,}860{,}000 \\
286{,}000 \\
28{,}600
\end{array}
$$

After taking out the maximum hundreds of 286, we have 19,400 left over.

We must now go to the tens' place.

The question to be asked in the tens' place is, "Can I take ten 286's out of 19,400?" (Yes)

Since we can take ten 286's out, perhaps we can take out twenty 286's; or thirty 286's; or forty 286's; and so on, up to ninety 286's.

In order to estimate the **maximum tens** of 286 we can take out, we use the first digit, 2, in the divisor and the first two digits, 19, in 19,400.

Since 2 goes into 19 eight times, we will see if we can take out eighty 286's (we cannot).

Since eighty 286's is too large, we will try to take out seventy 286's (we cannot).

Since seventy 286's is too large, we will try to take out sixty 286's (we can).

So the maximum tens of 286 we can take out is 6 (six tens).

After taking out the maximum tens of 286, we have 2,240 left over.

We must now go to the ones' place.

The question to be asked in the ones' place is, "Can I take one 286 out of 2,240?" (Yes)

The work now looks like this:

$$
\begin{array}{r}
36 \\
286\overline{)105{,}200} \\
-\ 85{,}800 \\
\hline
19{,}400 \\
-\ 17{,}160 \\
\hline
2{,}240
\end{array}
\qquad
\begin{array}{r}
28{,}600{,}000 \\
2{,}860{,}000 \\
286{,}000 \\
28{,}600 \\
2{,}860 \\
286
\end{array}
$$

Since we can take one 286 out, perhaps we can take out two 286's; or three 286's; or four 286's; and so on, up to nine 286's.

In order to estimate the **maximum ones** of 286 we can take out, we use the first digit, 2, in the divisor and the first digit, 2, in 2,240.

Since 2 goes into 2 once, we must consider whether this means one 286 or ten 286's.

To resolve this question, we must ask whether the 2,240 is closest to ten 286's or one 286.

Since 2,240 is closest to ten 286's, we will try to take out nine 286's (we cannot).

So we will try to take out eight 286's (we cannot).

So we will try to take out seven 286's (we can).

The maximum ones of 286 we can take out of 2,240 is 7 (seven ones).

The work finally looks like this:

$$
\begin{array}{r}
367 \\
286\overline{)105{,}200} \\
-\,85{,}800 \\
\hline
19{,}400 \\
-\,17{,}160 \\
\hline
2{,}240 \\
-\,2{,}002 \\
\hline
238
\end{array}
$$

28,600,000
2,860,000
286,000
28,600
2,860
286

Altogether, we have taken three hundred sixty-seven 286's out of 105,200 and we have 238 left over.

Have learners **check** their work by means of the following problem: If you take three hundred sixty-seven 286's out of a number and you have 238 left over, what is the number?

Have learners practice the examples of Facility Exercises #41 (Workbook II) to the level of facility; **then move on.**

SOLVING WORD PROBLEMS

Objective: Learners will solve word problems.

Write the following problem on the board:
> My principal has $497 and wishes to buy workbooks at $6 each. How many workbooks can she buy?

Have your learners solve this problem by the method described above. Learners conclude they can buy 82 workbooks and have $5 left over.

Now have the learners make up a word problem which checks the solution and confirms that it is correct.

Write the following problem on the board:
> My principal has $497 and buys 82 workbooks. How much did she pay for each workbook?

Write the following on the board:

$$82\overline{)497}$$

Have learners copy the example from the board.

Tell learners that the question associated with each place value, in the dividend, is different from those asked previously.
The reason for the difference is that the problem (above) does not ask us for the number of workbooks (which can be bought), but for the cost of each workbook.

The questions, according to place value, appear below.
1. Hundreds' place: Can we pay $100 for each workbook? (No)
2. Tens' place: Can we pay $10 for each workbook? (No)
3. Ones' place: Can we pay $1 for each workbook? (Yes)
Since we can pay $1 for each workbook, what are the maximum ones of dollars we can pay (for each workbook)?
By using the first digit, 8, in 82, and 49, in 497, we estimate that we can pay $6 for each workbook. Can we?

We find, eventually, that we could pay $6 for each workbook.
The board (and learners') work looks like this:

$$\begin{array}{r} 6 \\ 82\overline{)497} \\ -492 \\ \hline 5 \end{array}$$

If you pay $6 for each workbook, we have $5 left.

Can we pay more than $6 per workbook?

Elicit from learners that the maximum number of dollars we can pay for each workbook is $6.

The word problem which checks the solution above is:
If my principal buys 82 workbooks at $6 each, and has $5 left, how much money did she start with?

Have learners check the solution.

Write the following on the board:
The School Board has $11,498 to buy tables at $43 each. How many tables can they buy?

Have your learners solve this problem.

Learners conclude they can buy 267 tables and have $17 left over.

Now have them make up the word problem which checks the solution and confirms that it is correct.

Write the following problem on the board:
The School Board has $11,498 and buys 267 tables. What is the maximum they could pay for each table?

Write the following on the board:

$$267\overline{)11,498}$$

The questions, according to place value, appear below.
1. Can we pay $10,000 for each table? (No)
2. Can we pay $1,000 for each table? (No)
3. Can we pay $100 for each table? (No)
4. Can we pay $10 for each table? (Yes)

Since we can pay $10 for each table, what are the maximum tens of dollars we can pay (for each table)?

By using the first digit, 2, in 267, and 11, in 11,498, we estimate that we can pay $50 for each table. Can we?

We find, eventually, that we could pay $40 for each table.

The board (and learners') work looks like this:

$$
\begin{array}{r}
4 \\
267\overline{)11{,}498} \\
-10{,}680 \\
\hline
818
\end{array}
$$

If we pay $40 for each table, we have $818 left.

Can we pay more than $40 per table?

Continuing with the place value questions, we ask, "Can we pay $1 more for each table?" (Yes we can, since we have $818 left and paying $1 more per table would cost $267)

Since we can pay $1 more for each table, we use the first digit, 2, in 267, and the 8, in 818, to estimate that we can pay $4 more for each table. Can we? We find, eventually, that we can pay $3 more for each table.

The board (and learners') work finally looks like this:

$$
\begin{array}{r}
43 \\
267\overline{)11{,}498} \\
-10{,}680 \\
\hline
818 \\
-801 \\
\hline
17
\end{array}
$$

We conclude that the maximum cost of each table is $43, and there are $17 left over.

Have the learners make up the word problem for checking the above solution.

Have them check it.

It is very important to have learners see the relationship between word problems which require multiplication, and those which require division. Accordingly, have your learners compare the following problems:
1. Your principal buys 267 tables at $43 each and has $17 remaining. How much money did she have originally?
2. Your principal has $11,498 and wishes to buy tables at $43 each. How many tables can she buy? How much money does she have left?
3. Your principal as $11,498 and buys 267 tables. How much did she pay for each table? How much money does she have left?

Have learners discuss their solutions.

The use of word problems to make the steps of long division meaningful will enable learners to become skillful in both areas (word problems and long division).

Have learners practice the examples of Facility Exercises #42 (Workbook II) to the level of facility; **then move on.**

MULTIPLES

Objective: The learner will find all numbers of which a given number, between one and one hundred, is a multiple.

Give examples of the use of the word "multiple."
Here are some:
    "We say that 24 is a multiple of 6 because it is equivalent to 4 times 6."
    "We say that 24 is a multiple of 4 because it is equivalent to 6 times 4."
    "Is 24 a multiple of any other numbers?"
    "Why is 24 a multiple of 8?" (Because it is equivalent to 3 times 8)
    "Why is 24 a multiple of 3?"

Elicit from learners that 24 is also a multiple of 2, 12, 1 and 24.
    "Why is 24 a multiple of 1?" (Because it is equivalent to 24 times 1)
    "Why is 24 a multiple of 24?" (Because it is equivalent to 1 times 24)
    "Why is 24 a multiple of 12?"
    "Why is 24 a multiple of 2?"

You should insist that learners use the word "multiple", and answer questions with complete statements.

A typical example in the next set of exercises is as follows:
    70 is a multiple of _____
Learners are to find all numbers of which 70 is a multiple.
A systematic way of proceeding is described below.

Ask,
    "Is 70 a multiple of one?" (Yes)
    "So, 70 is also a multiple of ____ ?" (70)

Have learners copy the following from the board:

        70 is a multiple of of 1, _____ , 70.

Tell learners,
    "All the numbers of which 70 is a multiple are between 1 and 70."

"We asked if 70 is a multiple of one. So now we ask, 'Is 70 a multiple of 2?'"

Ask, "How can we find out if 70 is a multiple of 2?"

Elicit division of 70 by 2 as a way of knowing if 70 is a multiple of 2.

Have learners do the division themselves.

Have learners copy the following from the board:

70 is a multiple of 1, 2, _____, 35, 70.

Tell learners, "All the remaining numbers, of which 70 is a multiple, are between 2 and 35."

Ask, "So, what do we ask now?" (Is 70 a multiple of 3?)

Have learners do the long division themselves and conclude that 70 is not a multiple of 3.
Continuing similarly, learners conclude that 70 is not a multiple of 4.

Similarly, elicit that 70 is a multiple of 5 and 14.

70 is a multiple of 1, 2, 5, _____, 14, 35, 70.

Ask, "Where are the remaining numbers of which 70 is a multiple?" (Between 5 and 14)
Continuing similarly, learners conclude that 70 is not a multiple of 6.

Elicit that 70 is a multiple of 7 and 10.

Have learners copy the following from the board:

70 is a multiple of 1, 2, 5, 7, _____, 10, 14, 35, 70.

Ask, "Where are the remaining numbers of which 70 is a multiple?" (Between 7 and 10)

Elicit, by means of division, that 70 is not a multiple of 8 or 9.

Ask, "Seventy is a multiple of how many different numbers?" (Eight)

Have learners practice the examples of Facility Exercises #43 (Workbook II) to the level of facility; **then move on.**

FACTORS

Objective: The learner will find all factors of any number between one and one hundred.

Have learners learn the meaning of the word "factor", by seeing its relationship to the word "multiple."

Tell learners,
   "If 20 is a multiple of 5, then 5 is a factor of 20."
   "Name all the factors of 30." (1, 30, 2, 15, 3, 10, 5, 6)

You should insist that learners use the word "factor" often and properly in classroom dialogues.

Examples in the next set of exercises will require learners to find ALL factors of various numbers.

Proceed to elicit factors of 105, by the same systematic method described in the previous section.

Ask,
   "Is one a factor of 105?" (Yes)
   "Prove it."

Have learners write the following:

$$1, \text{_____}, 105$$

Ask,
   "Where are the remaining factors of 105?" (Between 1 and 105)
   "What do we try now?" (Try 2)
   "Is 2 a factor of 105?" (Learners must do the division to show that 2 is not a factor of 105)
   "Is 3 a factor of 105?" (After doing the division, learners conclude that 3 and 35 are factors of 105)

Learners write the following:

$$1, 3, \underline{\hspace{2cm}}, 35, 105$$

Ask,

"Where are the remaining factors of 105?" (Between 3 and 35)

"What do we try now?" (4)

"Is 4 a factor of 105?" (After the division of 105 by 4, learners conclude that 4 is not a factor of 105)

Continue similarly.

Learners finally write all factors of 105. See below.

$$1, 3, 5, 7, 15, 21, 35, 105$$

Have learners practice the examples of Facility Exercises #44 (Workbook II) to the level of facility; **then move on.**

Facility Exercises #45 are the fifth of nine Mixed Practice experiences for learners in Workbook II.

PRIME FACTORIZATION

Objectives: The learner will
>   (a) find the prime factorization of any number between one and one hundred.
>   (b) use that prime factorization to find all factors of that number.

Tell learners,
>   "The expression 'six times seven' is also referred to as 'the product of six and seven'."
>   "Another name for 'the product of 6 and 7' is 42."

You should insist that learners use the word "product" often and properly in classroom dialogues.

Tell learners, "Name two factors of 48 such that their product is equal to 48." (6 and 8)

Notice that 6 is a factor of 48 which produces two new factors, 2 and 3.
Eight is also a factor of 48 which produces two new factors, 2 and 4.
Again, 4 is a factor of 48 which produces two new factors, 2 and 2.
However, neither the factor 2 nor the factor 3 can produce two new factors.
Counting numbers which cannot produce two new factors are called **prime numbers**.
Since prime numbers 2 and 3 are also factors of 48, they are called **prime factors** of 48.
The "tree" below is a convenient way of diagramming prime factorization for beginners.

Follow the diagrams below, from left to right, and you will see how the tree "grows."

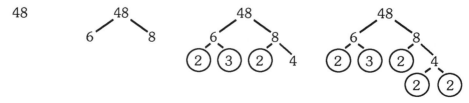

The prime factors are circled as soon as they show up. (A convenient practice for beginners)

When 48 is expressed as a **product** of its prime factors, we get

$$48 = 2x2x2x2x3.$$

Below are the trees for the prime factorization of 90, 70 and 15.

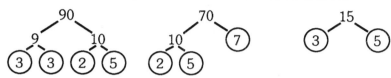

The prime factorizations are:

90 = 3x3x2x5
70 = 2x5x7
15 = 3x5

After sufficient written practice, you should have learners attempt to find the prime factorization of numbers (less than 100) mentally.

Have learners practice the examples of Facility Exercises #46 (Workbook II) to the level of facility; **then move on.**

FINDING ALL FACTORS OF A NUMBER
(by means of prime factorization)

Objective: The learner will use the prime factorization of a number to find all of its factors.

Write the prime factorization of 90 on the board. See below.

$$2 \times 3 \times 3 \times 5$$

Ask,

"Look at the prime factorization of 90. Do you see the factor 2 in it?"
"Is 2 a factor of 90?"

Place the illustration below on the board.

90

$$2 \times 3 \times 3 \times 5$$

$$2 \times 45$$

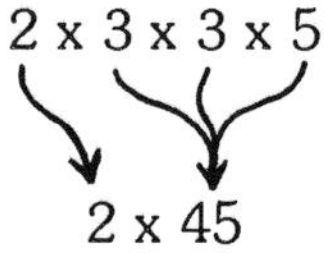

Tell learners, "This illustration shows that 2x45=90; so 2 and 45 are factors of 90."

Ask,

"Do you see the factor 3 in the prime factorization of 90?"
"Is 3 a factor of 90?"

Place the illustration below on the board.

90

$$2 \times 3 \times 3 \times 5$$

$$30 \times 3$$

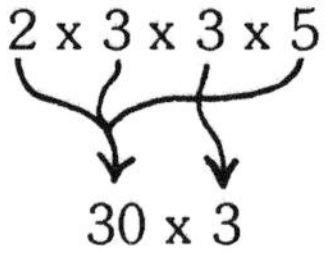

Tell learners, "This illustration shows that 3x30=90; so 3 and 30 are factors of 90."

Ask,

"Do you see the factor 5 in the prime factorization of 90?"
"Is 5 a factor of 90?"

Place the illustration on the board.

90

2 x 3 x 3 x 5

18

Tell learners, "This illustration shows that 18x5=90; so 5 and 18 are factors of 90."

Ask,

"Can you 'pick out' any more factors of 90 by just looking at its prime factorization?"
"Do you see 2x3 in the prime factorization of 90?"
"Is 6 a factor of 90?"
"Can you pick out any more factors of 90?"
"Do you see 2x5? 3x3? 3x5?"
"What is 2x5?" (10)
"What is 3x3? 3x5?"
"Are 10, 9 and 15 factors of 90?"

Place the illustrations below on the board.

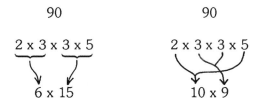

90   90

2 x 3 x 3 x 5   2 x 3 x 3 x 5

6 x 15   10 x 9

Tell learners, "These illustrations show that 6x15=90 and 10x9=90; so 6, 15, 10, and 9 are all factors of 90."

Ask,

"Do you see 2x3x3? 2x3x5? 3x3x5?"
"What is 2x3x3?" (18)
"What is 2x3x5?"
"What is 3x3x5?"

"Are 18, 30 and 45 factors of 90?"

"Of course you see 2x3x3x5. What is 2x3x3x5?" (90)

"Is 90 a factor of 90?"

Tell learners, "So the factors of 90 are 1, 2, 3, 5, 6, 9, 10, 15, 18, 30, 45, and 90."

Ask, "Did we leave out any factors of 90?"

Write the prime factorization of 32 on the board. See below.

$$2x2x2x2x2$$

Have learners pick out 2, 2x2 (or 4), 2x2x2 (or 8), 2x2x2x2 (or 16), 2x2x2x2x2 (or 32) as factors of 32.

Tell learners, "So the factors of 32 are 1, 2, 4, 8, 16, and 32."

Note that in the exercises below, learners are to find ALL factors of the given number.

Have learners practice the examples of Facility Exercises #47 (Workbook II) to the level of facility; **then move on.**

LEAST COMMON MULTIPLE

Objective: The learner will find the least common multiple of any two whole numbers between one and one hundred.

Copy the chart below on the board.

Numbers	Consecutive Multiples	Common Multiples	Least Common Multiple
2			
3			
3			
5			
4			
6			
9			
6			

Tell learners to name the first ten consecutive multiples of 2 (2, 4, 6, 8, 10, 12, 14, 16, 18, 20).

Fill in these first ten multiples of 2 on the chart.

Tell learners to name the first ten consecutive multiples of 3 (3, 6, 9, 12, 15, 18, 21, 24, 27, 30).

Fill in these first ten multiples of 3 on the chart.

Elicit responses from learners as follows:
"Examine the multiples of 2 and 3. Do you see any numbers which are in both sets of multiples?" (6, 12, 18)
"So 6, 12, and 18 are called common multiples of 2 and 3."
"Are 6, 12, and 18 the only common multiples of 2 and 3?"
"The only common multiples which your eyes see are 6, 12, and 18. Can you see any more with your minds?" (24, 30, 36, 42, 48, 54, 60, 66, 72, 78, 84,...)
"How many common multiples of 2 and 3 are there?" (Infinitely many)
"Of all the common multiples of 2 and 3, which one is the least?" (6)
"So 6 is the least common multiple (or L.C.M.) of 2 and 3."

The first rows of the chart can be filled in as appears below:

Numbers	Consecutive Multiples	Common Multiples	Least Common Multiple
2	2, 4, 6, 8, 10, 12, 14, 16, 18, 20,...	6, 12, 18, 24, 30, 36,...	6
3	3, 6, 9, 12, 15, 18, 21, 24, 27,30,...		

Note the use of the three dots in the chart above. The three dots to the right of 20, 30, and 36 indicate that each set of multiples has infinitely many members.

Using the same directions as above, elicit
(a) multiples,
(b) common multiples, and
(c) the least common multiple
of the following pairs of numbers: 3 and 5; 4 and 6; 9 and 6.

Fill in the remaining rows of the chart.

After completing the above exercises, have learners examine the sets of numbers under "Common Multiples."

Ask,
"The numbers 6, 12, 18, 24, 30, 36,...are multiples of what?"
"The numbers 15, 30, 45, 60, 75,...are multiples of what?"
"The numbers 12, 24, 36, 48, 60,...are multiples of what?"
"The numbers 18, 36, 54, 72,...are multiples of what?"

"In each case, the set of common multiples is a multiple of what?" (The L.C.M.)

Tell learners, "So as soon as we know the L.C.M., we also know all of the common multiples."

Have learners respond to the following:

The L.C.M. of 9 and 12 is 36. Find five more common multiples of 9 and 12.

The L.C.M. of 14 and 8 is 56. Find five more common multiples of 14 and 8.

The L.C.M. of 13 and 26 is 26. Find five more common multiples of 13 and 26.

Have learners practice the examples of Facility Exercises #48 (Workbook II) to the level of facility; **then move on.**

HIGHEST COMMON FACTOR

Objective: The learner will find the highest common factor of any two whole numbers between one and one hundred.

Copy the chart below on the board:

Numbers	ALL Factors	Common Factors	Highest Common Factor
18			
12			
36			
54			
80			
63			
82			
74			

Tell learners to name the factors of 18 (1, 2, 3, 6, 9, 18).

Fill in these factors of 18 on the chart.

Tell learners to name the factors of 12 (1, 2, 3, 4, 6, 12).

Fill in these factors of 12 on the chart.

Elicit responses from learners as follows:
"Examine the factors of 18 and 12. Do you see any numbers in both sets of factors?" (1, 2, 3, 6)
"So 1, 2, 3, and 6 are called common factors of 18 and 12."
"Are 1, 2, 3, and 6 the only common factors of 18 and 12?"

"How many common factors of 18 and 12 are there?"
"Of all the common factors of 18 and 12, which one is the highest?"
"So 6 is the highest common factor (or H.C.F.) of 18 and 12."

The first two rows of the chart can be filled in as appears below:

Numbers	ALL Factors	Common Factors	Highest Common Factor
18	1, 2, 3, 6, 9, 18	1, 2, 3, 6	6
12	1, 2, 3, 4, 6, 12		

Using the same approach as above, elicit all factors, common factors, and the highest common factor of the following pairs of numbers: 36 and 54; 80 and 63; 32 and 96; 82 and 74.

Fill in the remaining rows of the chart.

Have learners practice the examples of Facility Exercises #49 (Workbook II) to the level of facility; **then move on.**

Facility Exercises #50 are the sixth of nine Mixed Practice experiences for learners in Workbook II.

USING PRIME FACTORIZATION TO FIND THE L.C.M.

Objective: Given two whole numbers, the learner will use prime factorization to find the L.C.M.

Tell learners, "Look at the prime factorization of 24 and 90."

Write the following on the board and have learners copy in their notebooks:

24	90
2x2x2x3	2x3x3x5

Direct learners as follows:
"What factors does the prime factorization of 24 have which the prime factorization of 90 does not have?" (Two factors of 2)
"Place these extra factors on the right of the prime factors of 90 and underline them."
"What factors does the prime factorization of 90 have which the prime factorization of 24 does not have?" (One factor of 3 and one factor of 5)
"Place these extra factors on the right of the prime factors of 24 and underline them."

The work now looks like this:

24	90
2x2x2x3x<u>3x5</u>	2x3x3x5x<u>2x2</u>

"Now compare the set of prime factors below the 24 with the set of prime factors below the 90. Do you see that they both contain three factors of 2, two factors of 3, and one factor of 5?"
"Do you see that this process of 'swapping' extra factors gives us two sets of prime factors, which have the same factors?"
"The rest of the work now looks like this." (See below)

24	90
2x2x2x3x<u>3x5</u>	2x3x3x5x<u>2x2</u>
= 24 x 15	= 90 x 4
= 360	= 360

"Now 360 is equivalent to 15x24 and is also equivalent to 4x90."

"Consequently, 360 is a common multiple of 24 and 90."

"Is 360 the least common multiple of 24 and 90?"

"Look at the prime factorization of 360." (2x2x2x3x3x5)

"You can see that this set of prime factors, 2x2x2x3x3x5, contains within it the prime factors of 24."

"Do you also see the prime factors of 90 within the set of prime factors 2x2x2x3x3x5?"

"If we 'pick out' the prime factors of 24 from within 2x2x2x3x3x5, what's left?" (3x5)

"If we pick out the prime factors of 90 from within 2x2x2x3x3x5, what's left?" (2x2)

"So we can pick out the prime factors of 24 from within the set of factors 2x2x2x3x3x5, and after 'replacing' them, we can pick out the prime factors of 90."

"Now, if we were to take a single prime factor out of the set of factors 2x2x2x3x3x5, say a 3, for example, we could still pick out the prime factors of 24; but after 'replacing' them, could we still pick out the prime factors of 90?" (No)

Elicit from learners, through similar questions, that by taking out a 2, we could still pick out the prime factors of 90, but not those of 24.

Elicit from learners that by taking out the 5, we could still pick out the prime factors of 24, but not those of 90.

Ask, "If we remove a single factor from 2x2x2x3x3x5 will we still be able to pick out the prime factors of 24, and also the prime factors of 90?" (No)

Tell learners, "This is why 2x2x2x3x3x5, or 360, is **the least** common multiple of 24 and 90."

Use the same directions above to elicit the various steps in the model problems below.
Problem: Find the L.C.M. of 126 and 30.

Model of learners' work		**Rough work**
126	30	

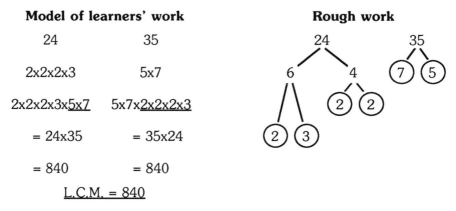

2x3x3x7	2x3x5
2x3x3x7x<u>5</u>	2x3x5x<u>3x7</u>
= 126x5	= 30x21
= 630	= 630

<u>L.C.M. = 630</u>

Another problem: Find the L.C.M. of 24 and 35.

Model of learners' work		**Rough work**
24	35	

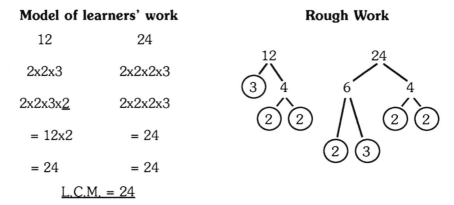

2x2x2x3	5x7
2x2x2x3x<u>5x7</u>	5x7x<u>2x2x2x3</u>
= 24x35	= 35x24
= 840	= 840

<u>L.C.M. = 840</u>

One more problem: Find the L.C.M. of 12 and 24.

Model of learners' work		**Rough Work**
12	24	
2x2x3	2x2x2x3	
2x2x3x<u>2</u>	2x2x2x3	
= 12x2	= 24	
= 24	= 24	

<u>L.C.M. = 24</u>

Have learners practice the examples of Facility Exercises #51 (Workbook II) to the level of facility; **then move on.**

USING PRIME FACTORIZATION TO FIND THE H.C.F.

Objective: Given two whole numbers, the learner will use prime factorization to find the H.C.F.

Lead learners through the following questions:
"If Linda has $5 does she have $1?" (Yes)
"If Linda has $5 does she have $2?" (Yes)
"If Linda has $5 does she have $3?" (Yes)
"If Linda has $5 does she have $4?" (Yes)
"If Linda has $5 does she have $5?" (Yes)
"If Linda has $5 does she have $6?" (No)
"If Linda has $5 does she also have less than $5?" (Yes)
"If Linda has $5 does she have more than $5?" (No)
"If Linda has $5 and Mark has $3, do they have $1 each? $2 each? $3 each? $4 each?"
"Since Linda and Mark have at most $3 each, we say that they have a maximum of $3 **in common**."
"If Keisha has $4 and Marcus has $7, what is the maximum amount that they have in common?" ($4)

Write the following on the board, and have learners copy in their notebooks:

  72   90

  2x2x2x3x3   2x3x3x5

Direct learners as follows:
"Look at the prime factorizations of 72 and 90."
"Since 72 has three factors of 2, and 90 has one factor of 2, what is the maximum number of 2's they have in common?" (One)
"Underline one 2 in the prime factorization of 72, and one 2 in the prime factorization of 90."
"Since 72 has two factors of 3, and 90 has two factors of 3, what is the maximum number of 3's they have in common?" (Two)

"Underline two 3's in the prime factorization of 72, and two 3's in the prime factorization of 90."

The board work now looks like this:

    72   90

2x2x2x<u>3x3</u>   <u>2x3x3</u>x5

"Multiply the factors of 72 which are underlined; what do you get?" (Eighteen)
"Multiply the factors of 72 which are not underlined; what do you get?" (Four)
"Multiply the factors of 90 which are underlined; what do you get?" (Eighteen)
"Are all factors of 90 underlined?"
"Which factors of 90 are not underlined?" (Five)

The board work now looks like this:

     72   90

2x2x2x<u>3x3</u>   <u>2x3x3</u>x5

  <u>18</u>x4   <u>18</u>x5

Ask, "Look at the board and tell me what is the highest common factor of 72 and 90?" (Eighteen)

Use the same directions above to elicit the various steps in the model problems below.

Problem: Find the H.C.F. of 32 and 36.

Model of learners' work   **Rough work**

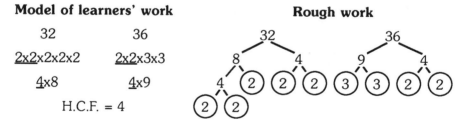

Another problem: Find the H.C.F. of 135 and 162.

Model of learners' work   **Rough work**

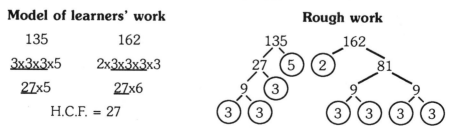

One more problem: Find the H.C.F. of 12 and 24.

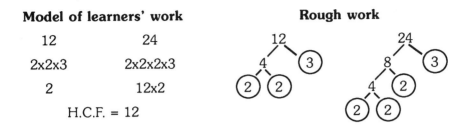

Model of learners' work		**Rough work**
12	24	
2x2x3	2x2x2x3	
2	12x2	
	H.C.F. = 12	

Have learners practice the examples of Facility Exercises #52 (Workbook II) to the level of facility; **then move on**.

INTRODUCTION TO FRACTIONS

Objective: The learner will name fractional parts of whole figures.

Draw a reasonable representation of the diagram below on the board:

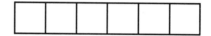

After drawing the figure, say to learners, "This rectangle has been divided into six equal slices. If they don't look equal, pretend they are."

Tell them you are going to ask two questions.
The first question is: How many equal slices?
The second question is: What are they called?

Emphasize the differences in the responses to both questions.
The answer to the first is **six**.
The answer to the second is **sixths**.

It is very important that you listen carefully to ensure that they respond, in the correct way, to each question.

Now erase the slice on the right of the figure.
  "How many equal slices now?" (Five)
  "What are these slices called?"(Fifths)
  "Why are they called fifths?" (Because there are **five equal** slices)

Now erase the slice on the right of the figure.
  "How many equal slices now?" (Four)
  "What are these slices called?" (Fourths)
  "Why are they called fourths?" (Because there are **four equal** slices)

Now erase the slice on the right of the figure.
  "How many equal slices now?" (Three)
  "What are these slices called?" (Thirds)

"Why are these slices called thirds?" (Because there are **three equal** slices)

Now erase the slice on the right of the figure.
"How many equal slices now?" (Two)
"What are these slices called?" (Halves)
"Why are these slices called halves?" (Because there are **two equal** slices)

Draw a reasonable representation of the diagram below on the board:

Ask,
"The rectangle above has been divided into how many equal slices?" (Ten)
"So what are the slices called?" (Tenths)
"How many tenths are shaded?" (Five)
"Five what?" (Tenths)
"So what part of the rectangle is shaded?" (Five-tenths)
"What part of the rectangle is not shaded?" (Five-tenths)
"What are five-tenths plus five-tenths?" (Ten-tenths)

Tell learners that ten-tenths equal the whole rectangle.

Write on the board and explain:

$$\frac{5}{10} + \frac{5}{10} = \frac{10}{10} = 1 \qquad \leftarrow \text{This means one whole (rectangle).}$$

Now erase the slice on the right of the rectangle.

See below for the resulting figure.

Ask,
"Are these slices still called tenths?"
"What are they called now?"
"How many ninths are shaded?" (Five)
"Five what?" (Five-ninths)
"So what part of the rectangle is shaded?" (Five-ninths)
"What part of the rectangle is not shaded?" (Four-ninths)
"What are five-ninths plus four-ninths?"

Tell learners that nine-ninths equal the whole rectangle.

Write on the board and explain.

$$\frac{5}{9} + \frac{4}{9} = \frac{9}{9} = 1$$ ← What does this mean? (One whole rectangle)

Now erase the slice on the right of the rectangle. See below for the resulting figure.

Ask,
"What are these slices called?"
"Why are they called eighths?"
"What part of the rectangle is shaded?"
"What part of the rectangle is not shaded?"
"What are five-eighths plus three-eighths?"
"And eight-eighths equal _____?" (The whole rectangle)

Write on the board:

$$\frac{5}{8} + \frac{3}{8} = \frac{8}{8} = 1$$ ← What does this mean?

Continue, similarly, erasing slices from the right side and asking the questions. As you proceed, learners will have no difficulty relating "seven" to "sevenths"; "six" to "sixths"; and "four" to "fourths."

Be sure learners say:
(a) fifths (not "fiveths") when there are five equal slices;
(b) thirds (not "threeths") when there are three equal slices; and
(c) halves (not "twoths") when there are two equal slices.

Place the following diagram on the board:

Ask, "Into how many equal parts is this circle divided?"

Elicit from learners that since there are four equal slices, the parts are named fourths.

Shade in three equal slices (see below).

Ask,

"In this circle, how many fourths are shaded?" (Three)

"So the part of the circle which is shaded is 'three-fourths.'"

"How many fourths are in the whole circle?" (Four fourths are in the whole circle)

Place the following diagram on the board:

Ask, "Into how many equal parts is this circle divided?"

Elicit from learners that since there are five equal slices, the parts are called fifths.

Label one slice with the letter y and two slices with the letter x (see below).

Ask,

"In this circle, how many fifths have x's in them?" (Two)

"So what is the part of the circle containing x's?" (Two-fifths)

"What is the part of the circle containing y?" (One-fifth)

"What is the part of the circle containing no letter?" (Two-fifths)

"How many fifths are in the whole circle?"

Introduce "fraction of" as another name for "part of."

Place the following diagrams on the board:

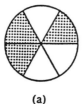 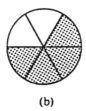 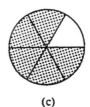 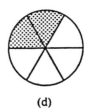

(a)　　　　　　(b)　　　　　　(c)　　　　　　(d)

Ask,

"In each circle, what is the name of the parts?" (Sixths)
"What fraction of circle (a) is shaded?"
"What fraction of circle (a) is not shaded?"
"What fraction of circle (b) is shaded?"
"What fraction of circle (b) is not shaded?"
"What fraction of circle (c) is shaded?"
"What fraction of circle (c) is not shaded?"
"What fraction of circle (d) is shaded?"
"What fraction of circle (d) is not shaded?"

Place the following diagrams on the board:

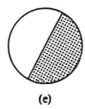 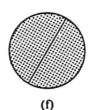

(e)　　　　　　　　(f)

Ask,

"In each circle, what is the name of the parts?" (Halves)
"What fraction of circle (e) is shaded?" (One-half)
"What fraction of circle (e) is not shaded?"
"What fraction of circle (f) is shaded?" (Two-halves)

Place the following diagrams on the board:

 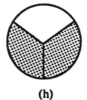 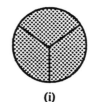

(g)　　　　　　(h)　　　　　　(i)

Ask,

"In each circle, what is the name of the parts?" (Thirds)
"What fraction of circle (g) is shaded?" (One-third)
"What fraction of circle (g) is not shaded?"
"What fraction of circle (h) is shaded?"
"What fraction of circle (h) is not shaded?"
"What fraction of circle (i) is shaded?"
"What fraction of circle (i) is not shaded?"
"How many thirds are in the whole circle?"

Ask,

"How many fifths in one whole?" (Five)
"So how many fifths are in two wholes?" (Ten)
"How many fifths are in three wholes? Four wholes?"

"How many thirds are in one whole?" (Three)
"So how many thirds are in two wholes?"
"How many thirds are in three wholes? Four wholes? Five wholes?"
"How many sixths in four wholes?"
"How many tenths in nine wholes?"
"Eight wholes, how many ninths?"
"Seven wholes, how many fourths?"
"Six wholes, how many halves?"
"Eight wholes, how many eighths?"

Have learners practice the examples of Facility Exercises #53 (Workbook II) to the level of facility; **then move on**.

FAMILIES OF EQUIVALENT FRACTIONS

Objectives: Given a fraction in lowest terms, the learner will
      (a) name many consecutive members of that family;
      (b) name the member of the family which corresponds to a particular ordinal number (for example, given a fraction in lowest terms such as two-sevenths, the learner will name the fifth member of its family);
      (c) tell which ordinal number corresponds to a particular member of a family (for example, learners will tell that the fraction eight twenty-eighths is the fourth member of the two-sevenths family); and
      (d) name the missing numerator or denominator of a family member, and the ordinal number corresponding to it.

Place the following diagram on the board:

Point out the 5 equal slices in the rectangle above.

Ask,
    "What are these slices called?" (Fifths)
    "What fraction of the rectangle is shaded?" (Three-fifths)

Now draw another rectangle beneath the one on the board and divide it into fifths (see below).

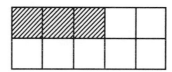

Tell learners, "In the lower rectangle, I am going to divide each fifth into two equal slices."

After dividing each fifth into two equal slices, the diagram will appear as below:

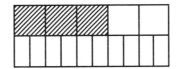

Tell learners, "When we divide fifths into two equal slices, what are the new slices called?" (Tenths)

Ask, "How many tenths are the same size as the three-fifths?"

Be sure each learner sees that six-tenths are exactly the same size as three-fifths.

Write on the board:

$$\frac{3}{5} = \frac{6}{10}$$

Be sure learners actually compare the **size** of the slice called one-fifth, with the size of the slice called one-tenth (see below).

Since five of these cover the top rectangle, this is one-fifth of the rectangle.

Since ten of these cover the top rectangle, this is one-tenth of the rectangle.

Ask, "Which is smaller; one-fifth or one-tenth?"

Now draw another rectangle beneath the two on the board, and divide it into fifths (see below).

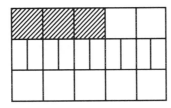

Tell learners, "In the bottom rectangle, I am going to divide each fifth into three equal slices."

After dividing each fifth into three equal slices, the diagram will appear as below:

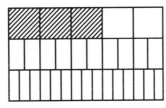

Tell learners, "When we divide fifths into three equal slices, what are the new slices called?" (Fifteenths)

Ask, "How many fifteenths make up the same length as the three-fifths?"

Be sure each learner sees that nine-fifteenths are exactly the same size as three-fifths, or six-tenths.

Write on the board:

$$\frac{3}{5} = \frac{6}{10} = \frac{9}{15}$$

Continue similarly with the diagram, dividing each fifth into 4 equal slices; then 5 equal slices.

Ask similar questions to those above.

Eventually the following should be written on the board:

$$\frac{3}{5} = \frac{6}{10} = \frac{9}{15} = \frac{12}{20} = \frac{15}{25}$$

Tell learners to take a good look at the fractions above.

Now ask, "What is the next one? The next? The next?"

Eventually, learners should have named many more fractions equivalent to 3/5 (see below).

$$\frac{3}{5} = \frac{6}{10} = \frac{9}{15} = \frac{12}{20} = \frac{15}{25} = \frac{18}{30} = \frac{21}{35} = \frac{24}{40} = \frac{27}{45} = \frac{30}{50} = \frac{33}{55} = \frac{36}{60} = \frac{39}{65} =$$
$$\frac{42}{70} = \frac{45}{75} = \frac{48}{80} = \ldots$$

Ask,
   "Is there another? And another? And another?"
   "Is there a 'last one'?"

Tell learners that the three dots mean "and so on in the same way."

Ask,
   "What does 'in the same way' mean?" (Adding 3 to the numerator of the last fraction and 5 to its denominator)
   "This set of fractions is called 'the three-fifth's family of equivalent fractions.'"
   "Since there is no 'last one' in the family, we say that the family has 'infinitely many' members."

By means of appropriate diagrams and dialogues similar to the above, elicit many other families of equivalent fractions, such as the following:

(a) the two-seventh's family;
(b) the three-fourth's family;
(c) the five-eighth's family; and
(d) the three-tenth's family.

Without diagrams, elicit from the learners the first ten members of the following families:

(a) $\dfrac{6}{7}$ (b) $\dfrac{2}{3}$ (c) $\dfrac{9}{10}$ (d) $\dfrac{1}{4}$ (e) $\dfrac{3}{4}$ (f) $\dfrac{5}{8}$ (g) $\dfrac{1}{3}$ (h) $\dfrac{1}{2}$

Elicit from the learners that
1. when each of the fifths of the rectangle was divided into two equal parts (or halves), it (the rectangle) was divided into tenths;
2. when each of the fifths of the rectangle was divided into three equal parts (or thirds), it (the rectangle) was divided into fifteenths; and
3. when each of the fifths of the rectangle was divided into four equal parts (or fourths), it (the rectangle) was divided into twentieths.

Consequently,
1. the halves of fifths are tenths;
2. the thirds of fifths are fifteenths; and
3. the fourths of fifths are twentieths.

What are the sevenths of fifths? (Thirty-fifths)
What are the twelfths of fifths? (Sixtieths)
What are the seventeenths of fifths? (Eighty-fifths)
What are the thirty-sixths of fifths? (One-hundred-eightieths)
What are the thousandths of fifths? (Five-thousandths)
What are the fourths of sevenths? (Illustrate, by means of a rectangle divided into seven equal parts, that if each seventh is divided into four equal parts, the whole rectangle is divided into twenty-eighths)
What are the sevenths of ninths? (Sixty-thirds)
What are the sixths of eighths? (Forty-eighths)
What are the halves of sevenths? (Fourteenths)
What are the tenths of thirds?
What are the thirds of tenths?
What are the fourths of fourths?

Continue to ask such questions, until learners respond confidently.

Have learners practice the examples of Facility Exercises #54 (Workbook II) to the level of facility; **then move on**.

Facility Exercises #55 are the seventh of nine Mixed Practice experiences in Workbook II.

Draw the following on the board:

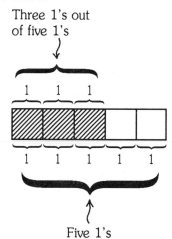

Three 1's out
of five 1's

Five 1's

Three out of five

$$\frac{3}{5}$$

=

Three 1's out of five 1's

$$\frac{3 \times 1}{5 \times 1}$$

Use the diagram above to show learners that three equal slices are shaded out of five.

Hence if we call each slice one (meaning one slice), then the three slices become "three ones", and the five slices become "five ones."

Consequently, the three-fifths shown above consist of three 1's out of five 1's.

Draw the following on the board:

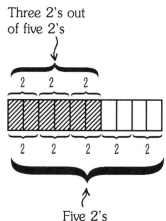

Three 2's out
of five 2's

Five 2's

Three out of five

$$\frac{3}{5}$$

=

Three 2's out of five 2's

$$\frac{3 \times 2}{5 \times 2}$$

Use the diagram above to show learners that the three shaded slices have become "three twos," and the five slices have become "five twos" (since each slice has become two equal parts).

Consequently, the three-fifths shown above consist of three 2's out of five 2's.

Draw the following on the board:

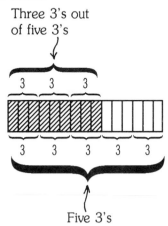

Three 3's out
of five 3's

Five 3's

Three out of five   Three 3's out of five 3's

$$\frac{3}{5} = \frac{3 \times 3}{5 \times 3}$$

In the diagram above, have learners see that the three slices have become "three threes," and the five slices have become "five threes" (since each slice has become three equal parts).
Consequently, the three-fifths shown above consist of three 3's out of five 3's.

Write on the board:

$$\frac{3\times1}{5\times1} = \frac{3\times2}{5\times2} = \frac{3\times3}{5\times3} = \frac{3\times4}{5\times4} = \frac{3\times5}{5\times5} = \frac{3\times6}{5\times6} = \ldots$$

$$\frac{3}{5} = \frac{6}{10} = \frac{9}{15} = \frac{12}{20} = \frac{15}{25} = \frac{18}{30} = \ldots$$

By means of the above, have learners see that the members of the three-fifth's family are all different examples of "three out of five."
For example, eighteen thirtieths are three sixes out of five sixes, while twenty-seven forty-fifths are three nines out of five nines.

Have learners see that the members of the five-eighth's family, for example, can be generated as follows:

$$\frac{5 \times 1}{8 \times 1} = \frac{5 \times 2}{8 \times 2} = \frac{5 \times 3}{8 \times 3} = \frac{5 \times 4}{8 \times 4} = \frac{5 \times 5}{8 \times 5} = \frac{5 \times 6}{8 \times 6} = \cdots$$

Have learners similarly generate many (at least ten) members of many families of equivalent fractions.

Have learners write the first ten members of the five-seventh's family.

Tell learners, "Look at the members of the five-seventh's family."

$$\frac{5}{7} = \frac{10}{14} = \frac{15}{21} = \frac{20}{28} = \frac{25}{35} = \frac{30}{42} = \frac{35}{49} = \frac{40}{56} = \frac{45}{63} = \frac{50}{70} = \cdots$$

Ask, "What can we do to the 5 and the 7, in 5/7, to get 30/42?" (Multiply each by 6)

Demonstrate to learners by means of the following diagram:

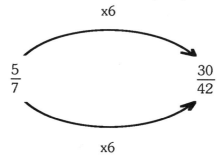

Ask, "What can we do to the 30 and the 42, in 30/42, to get back the 5/7?"

Demonstrate to learners by means of the following diagram:

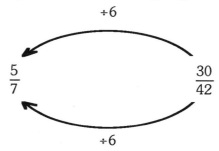

Ask,
   "What member of the 5/7 family is 30/42?" (The sixth)
   "What do you multiply the 5 and the 7 by in order to find the sixth member of the 5/7 family?" (Six)

   "What can we do to the 5 and the 7, in 5/7, to get 15/21?" (Multiply each by 3)

"What member of the 5/7 family is 15/21?" (The third)
"What do we multiply the 5 and the 7 by, in order to find the third member of the 5/7 family?" (Three)

"What member of the 5/7 family is 40/56?" (Eighth)
"What do we multiply the 5 and the 7 by, to find the eighth member of the 5/7 family?" (Eight)

"What must we multiply the 5 and the 7 by, to find the tenth member of the 5/7 family?"
"What is the tenth member of the 5/7 family?"

"What must we multiply the 5 and the 7 by, to find the fourteenth member of the 5/7 family?"
"What is the fourteenth member of the 5/7 family?"

"What is the eleventh member of the 5/7 family? The 15th? The 23rd? The l9th? The 2nd? The 37th? The 100th? The 263rd?"

"What member of the 5/7 family is 20/28?" (Fourth)
"What member of the 5/7 family is 35/49?" (Seventh)
"What member of the 5/7 family is 45/63?"
"What member of the 5/7 family is 65/91?"
"What member of the 5/7 family is 90/126?"
"What member of the 5/7 family is 115/161?"
"What member of the 5/7 family is 445/623?"
"What member of the 5/7 family is 205/287?"

"If 36/42 is the 6th member of a family, what is the first member?"
"If 18/21 is the 3rd member of a family, what is the first member?"
"If 72/84 is the 12th member of a family, what is the first member?"
"If 8/18 is the 2nd member of a family, what is the first member?"
"If 36/81 is the 9th member of a family, what is the first member?"
"If 78/143 is the 13th member of a family, what is the first member?"
"If 752/1,269 is the 47th member of a family, what is the first member?"

"Are there 28ths in the sevenths' family?" (Yes)
"Which member?" (The fourth)
"Are there forty-fifths in the sevenths' family?" (No)
"Are there eighteenths in the thirds' family?"
"Which member?"
"Are there twenty-fourths in the tenths' family?"
"Are there twenty-fourths in the eighths' family?"
"Which member?"
"Are there sixteenths in the halves' family?"
"Which member?"
"Are there fortieths in the sixths' family?"

"Are there fifty-fourths in the ninths' family?"
"Which member?"

Continue to ask many questions such as those above, until learners are responding confidently.

Have learners practice the examples of Facility Exercises #56 (Workbook II) to the level of facility; **then move on**.

Ask,
"What member of the 4/7 family is 12/____?" (The third)
"What is your way of knowing?"
"Fill in the missing number." (21)

"What member of the 5/9 family is ____/36?" (The fourth)
"What is your way of knowing?"
"Fill in the missing number." (20)

Have learners practice the examples of Facility Exercises #57 (Workbook II) to the level of facility; **then move on**.

Introduce the names "numerator" and "denominator" as follows below.

Draw the following on the board:

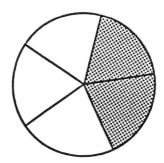

Tell learners:
"The circle above is divided into five equal parts."
"The number of parts which are shaded in the circle is two, and the name of each part is 'fifth.'"
"So, in the fraction two-fifths, the numeral at the top tells 'how many,' while the numeral at the bottom tells the name of the equal parts."
"The numeral which tells 'how many' is called the numerator, and is at the top of the fraction."
"The numeral which tells the name of the equal parts is called the denominator, and is at the bottom of the fraction."

REDUCING FRACTIONS TO LOWEST TERMS

Objective: The learner will reduce a fraction to lowest terms, by canceling or prime factorization.

Ask,

"If you are given 15/20 as a fraction in a certain family of equivalent fractions, can you find the first member of this family?"

"Which operation will you use to find it: addition, subtraction, multiplication, or division?"

Remind learners that they used division when they were given a member of a family and were asked to find the first member.

Ask, "What number would you divide both the 15 and the 20 by, in order to find the first member of the family to which 15/20 belongs?"

Have learners see that since 5 is a common factor of 15 and 20, we can find the first member as follows:

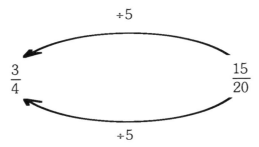

Tell learners that the process of finding the first member of the family, to which a given fraction belongs, is called "reducing a fraction to its lowest terms."

Be sure learners understand that when a fraction is "reduced," its value has not become smaller.

It is reduced in the sense that its numerator and denominator have become smaller, but the new fraction represents the **same number** as the original fraction.

Pose this problem: Reduce 24/36 to lowest terms.

Ask, "By what number can we divide both 24 and 36?"

If a learner offers "two" as an answer, accept it and illustrate the work on the board as follows:

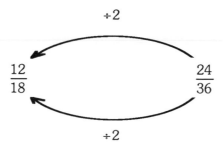

Ask, "Can 12/18 be reduced further?" "How?"

If a learner offers "two" as a divisor of 12 and 18, accept it and illustrate the work on the board as follows:

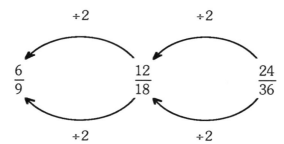

Ask, "Can 6/9 be reduced further?" "How?"

If a learner offers "three" as a divisor of both 6 and 9, illustrate the work on the board as follows:

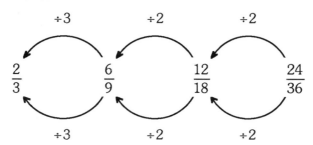

"Can we take 6/6 out of 23/6 four times?" (No)
"If we take 6/6 out of 23/6 three times, how many sixths are left over?" (Five-sixths)

Write on the board:

$$\frac{23}{6} = \underbrace{\frac{6}{6} + \frac{6}{6} + \frac{6}{6}}_{\downarrow} + \frac{5}{6}$$
$$3$$

Tell learners, "Since 6/6 equals one, then 23/6 equals 3 5/6."

By means of the above dialogues, have learners conclude as follows:

$$\frac{11}{4} = 2\frac{3}{4} \qquad\qquad \frac{47}{9} = 5\frac{2}{9} \qquad\qquad \frac{53}{8} = 6\frac{5}{8}$$

Write on the board:

$$\frac{37}{10}$$

We will now modify the above dialogues.

Ask,
   "How many tenths are equivalent to one?" (Ten)
   "Can we take one out of 37/10?"
   "How many tenths is that?" (Ten tenths)
   "Can we take two out of 37/10?" (Yes)
   "How many tenths is that?" (Twenty tenths)
   "Can we take three out of 37/10?" (Yes)
   "How many tenths is that?" (Thirty tenths)
   "Can we take four out of 37/10?" (No)
   "After taking three out of 37/10, how many tenths are left over?" (Seven tenths)
   "So 37/10 equals ____?" (3 7/10)

By means of the above dialogues, have learners conclude as follows:

$$\frac{14}{5} = 2\frac{4}{5} \qquad\qquad \frac{29}{6} = 4\frac{5}{6} \qquad\qquad \frac{19}{3} = 6\frac{1}{3}$$

Write on the board:

$$\frac{40}{9} \qquad \frac{32}{5} \qquad \frac{24}{7} \qquad \frac{12}{3} \qquad \frac{53}{10}$$

Ask, "How many ones can we take out of 40/9?" (Four)

Have learners explain why 40/9 = 4 4/9.

By asking how many ones they can take out, have learners do the remaining examples.

Tell learners that expressions such as 2 4/5, 4 5/6, and 6 1/3 are called "mixed numbers."

Below is a model of how a typical example in Facility Exercises #64 (Workbook II) is to be done.

Problem: Transform 27/8 to a mixed number.

Learner's work

$$\frac{27}{8} = \frac{8}{8} + \frac{8}{8} + \frac{8}{8} + \frac{3}{8}$$

$$\frac{27}{8} = 3\frac{3}{8}$$

Have learners practice the examples of Facility Exercises #64 to the level of facility; **then move on**.

We have seen that

$$\frac{32}{5} = 6\frac{2}{5}$$

$$\frac{24}{7} = 3\frac{3}{7}$$

$$\frac{12}{3} = 4$$

$$\frac{53}{10} = 5\frac{3}{10}$$

Elicit the usual short-cut for transforming improper fractions to mixed numbers, by means of the questions below.

"The improper fraction 32/5 'contains' 6 units."
"What can we do with the 32 and the 5, to get the 6?" (Divide 32 by 5)
"The improper fraction 24/7 contains 3 units."
"What can we do with the 24 and the 7, to get the 3?"
"The improper fraction 12/3 contains 4 units."

"What can we do with the 12 and the 3, to get 4?"
"The improper fraction 53/10 contains 5 units."
"What can we do with the 53 and the 10, to get the 5?"

Elicit that 23/4 = 5 3/4, by dividing 23 by 4, and placing the remainder over 4.

Have learners practice the examples of Facility Exercises #65 (Workbook II) to the level of facility; **then move on**.

TRANSFORMING MIXED NUMBERS
TO IMPROPER FRACTIONS

Objective: The learner will transform a mixed number to an improper fraction, and explain the transformation.

Lead learners through the following review:
  "Two wholes; how many thirds?"
  "Seven wholes; how many tenths?"
  "Four wholes; how many halves?"
  "Eight wholes; how many eighths?"
  "Ten wholes; how many tenths?"
  "Nine wholes; how many fifths?"

Continue to ask learners many similar questions.

Write on the board:

$$3\frac{2}{7} \qquad 7\frac{3}{8} \qquad 4\frac{1}{3} \qquad 1\frac{3}{4} \qquad 9\frac{1}{2} \qquad 6\frac{7}{10} \qquad 43\frac{23}{36}$$

Direct learners as follows:
  "Look at the mixed number 3 2/7."
  "The fractional part of 3 2/7 has sevenths."
  "Three wholes; how many sevenths?" (Twenty-one sevenths)
  "So 3 2/7 has how many sevenths?"

Write on the board:

$$3\frac{2}{7} = \frac{23}{7}$$

Have learners conclude that the mixed number 3 2/7 equals the improper fraction 23/7.

Direct learners as follows:
  "Look at the mixed number 7 3/8."
  "The fractional part of 7 3/8 has eighths."
  "Seven wholes; how many eighths?"

"So 7 3/8 has how many eighths?"

Have learners conclude that the mixed number 7 3/8 equals the improper fraction 59/8.

Similarly, have learners transform the remaining mixed numbers on the board to equivalent improper fractions.

Below is a model of how a typical example in Facility Exercises #66 (Workbook II) is to be done.

Problem: Transform 5 3/8 to an improper fraction.

Learner's work

$$5\frac{3}{8} = \frac{8}{8} + \frac{8}{8} + \frac{8}{8} + \frac{8}{8} + \frac{8}{8} + \frac{3}{8}$$

$$= \frac{43}{8}$$

Have learners practice the examples of Facility Exercises #66 to the level of facility; **then move on.**

Have learners see that

$$3 \times 7 + 2$$

$$3\frac{2}{7} = \frac{7}{7} + \frac{7}{7} + \frac{7}{7} + \frac{2}{7} = \frac{3 \times 7 + 2}{7} = \frac{23}{7}$$

Ask, "What can we do with the 3, the 7, and the 2 in 3 2/7, in order to end up with 23/7?" (Multiply 3 by 7 and add 2)

Again, have learners see that

$$5\frac{3}{8} = \frac{8}{8} + \frac{8}{8} + \frac{8}{8} + \frac{8}{8} + \frac{8}{8} + \frac{3}{8} = \frac{5 \times 8 + 3}{7} = \frac{43}{8}$$

Ask,
   "What can we do with the 5, the 8, and the 3 in 5 3/8, in order to end up with 43/8?"
   "The usual short-cut for transforming 5 3/8 to a mixed number is to multiply the 5 by the 8, add the 3, and place this result over 8." (43/8)

Have learners practice the examples of Facility Exercises #67 (Workbook II) to the level of facility; **then move on.**

ADDING AND SUBTRACTING WITH MIXED NUMBERS

Objectives: The learner will
(a) add and subtract with mixed numbers;
(b) check the answers to the subtraction examples; and
(c) do additions and subtractions, in which one number is a whole number and the other is a proper fraction or mixed number.

Write on the board:

$$7\frac{3}{8}$$
$$+\ 5\frac{1}{6}$$

Tell learners, "Anyone who can add 3/8 + 1/6 can also add 7 3/8 + 5 1/6."

Ask,
"Can you add the 3/8 + 1/6?" (Yes)
"Can you add the 7+5?" (Yes)

Tell learners, "First we will add the fractions. This means we must find the L.C.D."

Ask, "What is the L.C.D.?" (24)

The work should now appear on the board as follows:

$$7\frac{3}{8} = 7\frac{}{24}$$
$$+\ 5\frac{1}{6} = 5\frac{}{24}$$

Have learners notice that the whole numbers 7 and 5 are carried over to the next step.

Complete the work as follows:

$$7\frac{3}{8} = 7\frac{9}{24}$$

$$+\ 5\frac{1}{6} = 5\frac{4}{24}$$

$$12\frac{13}{24} \quad 12\frac{13}{24}$$

Explain the remaining steps of the example.

Be sure learners write the answer, 12 13/24, beneath the original example, 7 3/8 + 5 1/6.

This is important, since we do want the answer to 7 3/8 + 5 1/6.

Write on the board:

$$2\frac{3}{10}$$
$$+\ 7\frac{1}{5}$$

$$8\frac{1}{3}$$
$$+\ \ \frac{2}{5}$$

$$9\frac{5}{12}$$
$$+\ 9\frac{3}{8}$$

$$\frac{1}{2}$$
$$+\ 5\frac{1}{3}$$

$$\frac{3}{4}$$
$$+\ 12\frac{1}{6}$$

$$29\frac{29}{56}$$
$$+\ 37\frac{2}{7}$$

$$87\frac{4}{9}$$
$$+\ 59\frac{29}{63}$$

$$3\frac{5}{8}$$
$$+\ \ \frac{1}{6}$$

Have learners attempt each of the examples above. Assist them where necessary.

Write on the board:

$$15\frac{7}{10}$$
$$+\ 23\frac{5}{6}$$

Have learners proceed with the above on their own. Assist them where necessary.

Eventually, learners' work should appear as below.

$$15\frac{7}{10} = 15\frac{21}{30}$$
$$+\ 23\frac{5}{6} = 23\frac{25}{30}$$
$$38\frac{46}{30}$$

Tell learners to look at the answer 38 46/30.

Ask,

"What type of fraction is 46/30?" (Improper fraction)
"We can transform an improper fraction into a _____?"
"What mixed number will 46/30 give us?" (1 16/30)
"What can we do with the fraction 16/30?" (Reduce it to the lowest terms)
"Reduce 16/30 to lowest terms." (8/15)

Write on the board and explain.

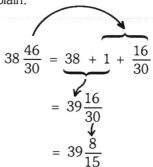

$$38\frac{46}{30} = 38 + 1 + \frac{16}{30}$$

$$= 39\frac{16}{30}$$

$$= 39\frac{8}{15}$$

Finally, learners' work should appear as below.

$$15\frac{7}{10} = 15\frac{21}{30}$$

$$+\ 23\frac{5}{6} = 23\frac{25}{30}$$

$$39\frac{8}{15} \qquad 38\frac{46}{30} = 39\frac{16}{30} = 39\frac{8}{15}$$

Be sure learners write the answer, 39 8/15, beneath the original example 15 7/10 + 23 5/6.

Write on the board:

$$5\frac{4}{7} \qquad\qquad 2\frac{3}{4} \qquad\qquad 27\frac{8}{13} \qquad\qquad \frac{7}{9}$$

$$+\ 1\frac{16}{21} \qquad\quad +\ 2\frac{5}{6} \qquad\quad +\ 6\frac{10}{13} \qquad\quad +\ 9\frac{5}{6}$$

$$6\frac{8}{9} \qquad\qquad 1\frac{19}{27} \qquad\qquad 8\frac{2}{3} \qquad\qquad \frac{7}{8}$$

$$+\ 4\frac{7}{9} \qquad\quad +\ \frac{5}{9} \qquad\qquad +\ 8\frac{5}{6} \qquad\quad +\ \frac{7}{8}$$

Have learners attempt each of the examples above.
Assist them where necessary.

Write on the board:

$$8\frac{2}{3}$$
$$-5\frac{7}{15}$$

Tell learners, "Anyone who can subtract 7/15 from 2/3, can also subtract 5 7/15 from 8 2/3."

Ask,
"Can you subtract 7/15 from 2/3?"
"Can you subtract 5 from 8?"

Tell learners, "First we will subtract with the fractions. This means we must find the L.C.D."

Have learners proceed on their own.
Assist them where necessary.

Eventually, their work should appear as below.

$$8\frac{2}{3} = 8\frac{10}{15}$$
$$-5\frac{7}{15} = 5\frac{7}{15}$$
$$3\frac{1}{5} \qquad 3\frac{3}{15} = 3\frac{1}{5}$$

Ask, "What can we do with the fraction 3/15?" (Reduce it to 1/5)

Be sure learners write the answer, 3 1/5, beneath the original example 8 2/3 – 5 7/15.

Ask, "If 3 1/5 is the answer to 8 2/3 – 5 7/15, how will we check it?"

Have learners see that if 8 2/3 – 5 7/15 = 3 1/5, it follows that 3 1/5 + 5 7/15 should be equal to 8 2/3.

Have learners do this addition.

Eventually, the work should appear as follows:

Check

$$5 \frac{7}{15} = 5 \frac{7}{15}$$

$$+ 3 \frac{1}{5} = 3 \frac{3}{15}$$

$$8 \frac{2}{3} \qquad 8 \frac{10}{15} = 8 \frac{2}{3}$$

Tell learners, "Since we 'get back' 8 2/3, the answer, 3 1/5, is correct."

Write on the board:

$$6 \frac{5}{9} \qquad\qquad 8 \frac{3}{4} \qquad\qquad 10 \frac{7}{10} \qquad\qquad 16 \frac{5}{7}$$

$$- 6 \frac{2}{9} \qquad\qquad - 3 \frac{1}{2} \qquad\qquad - 4 \frac{2}{5} \qquad\qquad - 9 \frac{1}{4}$$

$$13 \frac{5}{6} \qquad\qquad 5 \frac{2}{3} \qquad\qquad 7 \frac{4}{5} \qquad\qquad 2 \frac{1}{3}$$

$$- 2 \frac{3}{10} \qquad\qquad - \frac{1}{2} \qquad\qquad - 4 \frac{2}{3} \qquad\qquad - 2 \frac{1}{4}$$

Have learners attempt the examples above.
Assist them where necessary.

Be sure to have them check their answers.

Have learners practice the examples of Facility Exercises #68 (Workbook II) to the level of facility; **then move on**.

Illustrate and explain the following on the board:

$$4 \frac{2}{9} = 3 + 1 + \frac{2}{9}$$

$$= 3 + \frac{9}{9} + \frac{2}{9}$$

$$= 3 + \frac{11}{9}$$

$$4 \frac{2}{9} = 3 \frac{11}{9}$$

Be sure learners understand why 4 2/9 = 3 11/9.

Similarly lead learners through the following:

$$5\frac{3}{7} = 4\frac{10}{7} \qquad\qquad 1\frac{7}{8} = \frac{15}{8}$$

$$9\frac{5}{6} = 8\frac{11}{6} \qquad\qquad 7\frac{1}{3} = 6\frac{4}{3}$$

Have learners practice filling in the missing numerators and denominators below.

$$10\,\frac{2}{5} = 9 - \qquad\qquad 2\,\frac{1}{2} = 1 -$$

$$8\,\frac{9}{14} = 7 - \qquad\qquad 3\,\frac{3}{4} = 2 -$$

$$13\,\frac{9}{14} = 12 - \qquad\qquad 11\,\frac{1}{10} = 10 -$$

Have learners practice the examples of Facility Exercises #69 (Workbook II) to the level of facility; **then move on**.

Write the following on the board:

$$7\frac{3}{8}$$
$$-\;2\frac{5}{6}$$

Have learners do as much of this example as they can. They will be able to take it up to this point. (See below)

$$7\frac{3}{8} = 7\frac{9}{24}$$
$$-\;2\frac{5}{6} = 2\frac{20}{24}$$

Ask,
  "Can we subtract 20 twenty-fourths from 9 twenty-fourths?"
  "Are there enough twenty-fourths at the top, so that we can take away 20 twenty-fourths?" (No. There are only 9 twenty-fourths)
  "So at the top we need more _____?" (Twenty-fourths)

Be sure the need for more twenty-fourths, "at the top," is well understood in the learners' minds.

155

Ask, "How will we get more twenty-fourths?"

Carefully explain to learners that we can take 1 from the 7 (next to 9/24), and transform it to 24 twenty-fourths.

Demonstrate on the board as follows:

$$7\frac{9}{24} = 6 + 1 + \frac{9}{24}$$

$$7\frac{9}{24} = 6 + \frac{24}{24} + \frac{9}{24}$$

$$7\frac{9}{24} = 6 + \frac{33}{24}$$

$$7\frac{9}{24} = 6\frac{33}{24}$$

Learners' work should now appear as follows:

$$7\frac{3}{8} = 7\frac{9}{24} = 6\frac{33}{24}$$
$$-2\frac{5}{6} = 2\frac{20}{24} = 2\frac{20}{24}$$

Ask,

"Do we now have enough twenty-fourths at the top?"

"Can we take 20 twenty-fourths out of 33 twenty-fourths?" (Yes, 13 twenty-fourths are left)

Learners should complete the work as follows:

$$7\frac{3}{8} = 7\frac{9}{24} = 6\frac{33}{24}$$
$$-2\frac{5}{6} = 2\frac{20}{24} = 2\frac{20}{24}$$
$$4\frac{13}{24} \qquad 4\frac{13}{24}$$

Note, once again, that the answer, 4 13/24, is placed directly beneath the original example 7 3/8 – 2 5/6.

Ask, "If 4 13/24 is the answer to 7 3/8 – 2 5/6, how will we check it?"

Have learners see that if 7 3/8 – 2 5/6 = 4 13/24, it follows that 4 13/24 + 2 5/6 should be equal to 7 3/8.

The check should appear as follows:

$$\textbf{Check}$$

$$2\,\frac{5}{6} = 2\,\frac{20}{24}$$

$$+\,4\,\frac{13}{24} = 4\,\frac{13}{24}$$

$$7\,\frac{3}{8} \qquad 6\,\frac{33}{24} = 7\,\frac{9}{24} = 7\,\frac{3}{8}$$

Tell learners, "Since we get back 7 3/8, the answer, 4 13/24, is correct."

Write on the board:

$$6\,\frac{2}{9} \qquad\qquad 8\,\frac{1}{2} \qquad\qquad 10\,\frac{2}{5} \qquad\qquad 16\,\frac{1}{4}$$

$$-\,5\,\frac{5}{9} \qquad\qquad -\,3\,\frac{3}{4} \qquad\qquad -\,4\,\frac{7}{10} \qquad\qquad -\,9\,\frac{1}{3}$$

$$13\,\frac{3}{10} \qquad\qquad 5\,\frac{1}{2} \qquad\qquad 7\,\frac{2}{3} \qquad\qquad 1\,\frac{1}{10}$$

$$-\,2\,\frac{5}{6} \qquad\qquad -\,\frac{2}{3} \qquad\qquad -\,4\,\frac{4}{5} \qquad\qquad -\,\frac{1}{8}$$

Have learners attempt each of the examples above.
Assist them where necessary.

Be sure to have them check their answers.

Have learners practice the examples of Facility Exercises #70 (Workbook II) to the level of facility; **then move on**.

Review finding the L.C.M. by means of prime factorization.

Write on the board:

$$7\,\frac{23}{28}$$

$$+\,4\,\frac{13}{24}$$

Have learners attempt to find the L.C.D. by looking at multiples of the larger denominator (28).

They will soon conclude that this is a rather burdensome exercise.

Ask, "Can we find the L.C.D. by some other method?" (By means of prime factorization)

Have learners find the L.C.M. of 28 and 24. (See below)

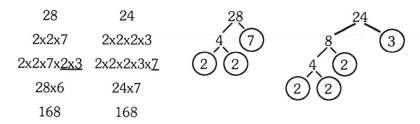

28	24
2x2x7	2x2x2x3
2x2x7x<u>2x3</u>	2x2x2x3x<u>7</u>
28x6	24x7
168	168

Tell learners, "The L.C.M. of 28 and 24 is 168. It is also the L.C.D. of the two fractions."

Now write the following on the board:

$$7\frac{23}{28} = 7\frac{138}{168}$$
$$+ 4\frac{13}{24} = 4\frac{91}{168}$$

Direct learners as follows:
   "One-hundred-sixty-eighths are what members of the 28ths family?" (The 6th. We see above that 28x6=168)
   "So fill in the numerator." (138)

   "One-hundred-sixty-eighths are what members of the 24ths family?" (The 7th. We see above that 24x7=168)
   "So fill in the numerator." (91)

Have learners complete the addition. (See below)

$$7\frac{23}{28} = 7\frac{138}{168}$$
$$+ 4\frac{13}{24} = 4\frac{91}{168}$$
$$12\frac{61}{168} \quad 11\frac{229}{168} = 12\frac{61}{168}$$

Write on the board:

$$8\frac{31}{48} \qquad 9\frac{41}{45} \qquad 7\frac{5}{18} \qquad 2\frac{33}{40}$$
$$-\ 8\frac{23}{30} \qquad -\ 6\frac{9}{20} \qquad +\ 2\frac{7}{24} \qquad +\ 3\frac{19}{28}$$

Lead learners through the above examples.

Write on the board:

(1)	(2)	(3)	(4)	(5)
7	$8\frac{2}{9}$	$8\frac{2}{9}$	$6\frac{7}{10}$	7
$-\ 3\frac{3}{5}$	$-\ 3$	$+\ 3$	$-\ \frac{3}{10}$	$+\ \frac{3}{5}$

Have learners look at example (1).

Ask,

"We have to take away three-fifths. Do you see any fifths at the top?"

"We need some fifths at the top, so we can take away three-fifths. How will we get some fifths at the top?" (Take 1 from 7 and transform it to five-fifths)

Learners complete work as appears below.

Check

$$7 \quad = 6\frac{5}{5} \qquad\qquad 3\frac{3}{5}$$
$$-\ 3\frac{3}{5} = 3\frac{3}{5} \qquad\qquad +\ 3\frac{2}{5}$$
$$\overline{}3\frac{2}{5} \quad 3\frac{2}{5} \qquad\qquad \overline{}6\frac{5}{5} = 7$$

Have learners look at example (2).

Ask, "Do you see something at the top which we can take 3 from?" (The 8)

Learners complete work as appears below.

$$8\frac{2}{9}$$
$$-\ 3$$
$$\overline{}$$
$$5\frac{2}{9}$$

Check

$$3$$
$$+\ 5\frac{2}{9}$$
$$\overline{}$$
$$8\frac{2}{9}$$

Have learners look at example (3).

Ask, "What is the answer?" (11 2/9)

Have learners look at example (4).

Ask, "What is the answer?"

Learners complete work as appears below.

$$6\frac{7}{10}$$
$$-\ \frac{3}{10}$$
$$\overline{\phantom{-\ \frac{3}{10}}}$$
$$6\frac{4}{10} = 6\frac{2}{5}$$

Check

$$\frac{3}{10} \qquad \frac{3}{10}$$
$$+\ 6\frac{2}{5} = 6\frac{4}{10}$$
$$\overline{\phantom{+\ 6\frac{2}{5}}}$$
$$6\frac{7}{10} \qquad 6\frac{7}{10}$$

Have learners look at example (5).

Ask, "What is the answer?" (7 3/5).

Have learners practice the examples of Facility Exercises #71 (Workbook II) to the level of facility; **then move on to Book III.**

Facility Exercises #72 are the ninth of nine Mixed Practice experiences for learners in Workbook II.